Style Your Soul

Get Dressed From The Inside Out!

Second Edition

Brittany Davis

-Founder & Editor-in-Chief, Virtuous Magazine

Published in the United States of America.

www.virtuousmagazine.com

Printed in the United States of America.

10 9 8 7 6 5 4 3 2 1

Second Edition

CONNECTING

For everything about this book and extra goodies visit:

www.virtuousmagazine.com

Find me and a whole community of like minded women on Facebook:

Facebook.com/virtuousmagazine

Instagram @Virtuousmagazine

If pinning is the name of your game follow Virtuous Magazine on Pinterest at **Pinterest.com/virtuousmagazine**

Let this book be the beginning of a wonderful friendship; sign up for the FREE weekly email devotionals online at **virtuousmagazine.com.**

Other titles by Brittany Davis: www.VirtuousMagazine.com

Style Your Soul Teacher's Guide

Style Your Heart: 31 Days To Loving Like The Lord

The Everyday Lady: Social Graces For Today's Social World

Ladies Day Themes

Thursday's Thought: Bible Advice For Everyday Life

To: God, Willie, Mom, Dad
and You!

Table of Contents

Part 1: Choose

Part 2: Walking Worthy

Part 3: Wardrobe

Hello, Hello! I'm so happy that you're here and that you've decided to join me on this journey of styling our souls!

Style Your Soul is a brand new way of thinking about you're life and how you're living it.

Girls and women who've styled their souls know that life has less to do with what's in our culture and more to do with what's in our heart.

This book will be your guide to dressing the hidden person of your heart. We'll start with choosing, because our lives are defined by the choices we make. We'll get really clear on the blessing that we get to choose everything.

Then we'll dive straight into transforming ourselves from the inside out by being living sacrifices every day. We'll check our friends and intentions in the mirror of the Word.

Finally we'll wrap up our metamorphosis by styling ourselves outwardly. We're jumping in with both feet to master our closets, learn how to shop like a pro and understand our purpose for getting dressed no matter the occasion.

I'm thrilled to pieces that you're ready to join in and *Style Your Soul*! I hope that you learn a lot, take life changing action and encourage even more sisters.

With all my love,

Brittany

Part I
Choose

Chapter 1

A Virtuous View

As children we all have big dreams, hopes and goals for our lives. We dream of our careers as we are asked, "What do you want to be when you grow up?" We dream of our wedding day and the man we will share our life with forever. We even dream about the house we'll live in, the car we'll drive and the places we'll visit.

And our visions are usually lofty. I mean I always imagined myself in France strolling the Champs Elysee. And having a vision is important; it's hard to get to a destination without a map. But visions don't always turn out as expected.

Life choices can take us down very winding and different paths than the ones we had in mind. Sometimes those paths lead us astray or sometimes a different path can lead us somewhere we love but didn't know we wanted to be.

I always imagined myself as a business woman, running some corporation, wearing power suits and looking over the city from my corner office window. And while I pursued that path and worked at a magazine, at a newspaper distribution office and at the Department of Juvenile Justice; I ultimately found fulfillment and contentment running a small business as a stay at home mom.

Your life will take many twists and turns and there will be bumps and bruises along the way. But the best news of all is that you have been blessed with free will. You get to choose. You get to choose everything.

You get to choose where or if you go to college, if or how many children you have, your spouse, where you live, how you work and how you serve. And while envisioning the stuff we wanted as children was fun, as we get older it's easy to see that what really matters is envisioning the person you want to be.

Because we all know that at the end of the day it doesn't really matter how big your house is or what car you drive; what matters is the character of your heart. We all want to be the kind of girls and women that others enjoy being around.

We want to build people up with kind words, we want to choose gratitude over complaining and we want to be remembered as the Virtuous Woman in Proverbs 31:29-30 which says, "Many daughters have done well, but you excel them all. Charm is deceitful and beauty is passing, but a woman who fears the Lord, she shall be praised."

Legacy

One of my favorite ways to make sure that I am constantly choosing the person I want be is to imagine myself at eighty years old looking back over my life. What was my life about? Was it about striving for cultural acceptance, being a boss or hoarding as many things as possible? And what do I have to show for it?

If I am blessed to see eighty years I know I'll want to be surrounded by my children and grand-children and great grand-children. I'll want to still be serving the best I can, I'll want my husband beside me and I'll want to experience the joy of a life spent walking beside my Savior. Did you notice that my desired vision of eighty never mentioned any possessions? 1 Tim. 6:6-8 says, “Now godliness with contentment is great gain. For we brought nothing into this world, and it is certain we can carry nothing out. And having food and clothing, with these we shall be content.”

What Is Your Vision Of Your Life At Eighty?

Now I can’t get to that vision of eighty without living out some key principles of life right now. I am already married to a wonderfully God fearing man, but if you aren’t yet married; have you taken into account the kind of man you want to marry? And have you thought about the kind of woman he’d like to marry?

We are very quick to rattle off the qualifications our future spouse will need to possess to have the privilege of marrying us, but many of us aren’t taught to give any thought to the kind of woman that he would want to marry.

For instance, let’s say your list contains the following qualifications: spiritual, handsome, smart, kind, courageous, supportive, hard working, funny, adventurous and a family man. And let’s say you found that man and were interested in beginning a relationship with him. What do you think is on his list of qualifications for a wife?

Do you think he’d want a wife that was lazy, a whiner, promiscuous, petty, brash or selfish? So many girls and women love to say things like, “Well this is how I am take it or leave it,” but they envision a life with a man who is good and kind hearted.

He’s going to want someone with a gentle and kind spirit. Someone who is loving, patient, hard working, smart, considerate, beautiful inside and out and spiritual.

God who gave us the opportunity to choose also arranged blessings and consequences for our choices. Every choice we make now will have a positive or negative effect on the life we want at eighty.

And as I mentioned before I am already married but that doesn't get me off the hook. If I want my husband smiling beside me, sharing in the joy of our family that won't happen by accident. I have to choose to honor him, love him and follow his lead in all of the years leading up to eighty.

If I want to be surrounded by my children and their children I have to be the kind of mother now who loves, nurtures, trains and teaches them. I cannot put them on the back burner chasing after the things our culture deems important. I used to believe whole heartedly that I had to be a girl boss to be important, that I couldn't make a difference if I wasn't out in the world forging my path and leading some empire.

And that is no slight to women who work outside the home, my issue wasn't necessarily the work but my heart. I honestly, truly couldn't see the value of being home with my children over building an empire. And yes on paper it sounds terrible and honestly I felt terrible. And it wasn't until I looked at the choices I'd made and submitted myself to God's plan that my heart began to heal.

My children didn't ask to be brought into this world. My husband and I made that choice. I made myself a mother and now it was my responsibility to live the way God would have mothers live.

Titus 2:4-5 says, "That they admonish the young women to love their husbands, to love their children, to be discreet, chaste, homemakers, good, obedient to their own husbands, that the word of God may not be blasphemed."

And I can only speak to my specific circumstances, yours may be different, but the truth is I can't be surrounded by a family when I'm eighty if I don't provide for them today.

Maybe your vision of your life at eighty has you in a specific place. What can you do now to ensure you'll be there? Perhaps your vision does include some things, which is fine too, how are you working towards them today?

Our visions are guaranteed to change shape and form as we get older, grow in grace and learn new things, but our choices will remain ours and they will either bring us closer to our vision or change it completely.

Role Models

Our culture loves reality tv stars and celebrities. They encourage us to look like them, act like them and buy the things they promote. But many of these women rose to fame in some very ungodly ways. And the lives they lead hardly will be remembered with joy and pride when they are eighty.

So why are many of these same women our role models? We can get caught up in the false glamour they exude and sometimes we want to look like them and have the things they own. But when we step back and take a look at our vision, it's clear that we need a different role model. We need someone to look up to who walked her path, focused on what mattered and whose legacy is one that women everywhere can admire.

There are many worthy women in the Bible whose life and legacy could be mentioned, but the one that has had the most profound impact on my life is that of the Virtuous woman of Proverbs 31. We briefly discussed her legacy, but let's look at the way she is described, her character and her life and see if we couldn't put her in the running for America's Next Top Role Model!

Proverbs 31:10-31 reads,

"Who can find a virtuous wife? For her worth is far above rubies. The heart of her husband safely trusts her; so he will have no lack of gain. She does him good and not evil all the days of her life. She seeks wool and flax, and willingly works with her hands. She is like the merchant ships, she brings her food from afar.

She also rises while it is yet night, and provides food for her household, and a portion for her maidservants. She considers a field and buys it; from her profits she plants a vineyard. She girds herself with strength, and strengthens her arms. She perceives that her merchandise is good, and her lamp does not go out by night.

She stretches out her hands to the distaff, and her hand holds the spindle. She extends her hand to the poor, yes, she reaches out her hands to the needy. She is not afraid of snow for her household, for all her household is clothed with scarlet. She makes tapestry for herself; her clothing is fine linen and purple. Her husband is known in the gates, when he sits among the elders of the land.

She makes linen garments and sells them, and supplies sashes for the merchants. Strength and honor are her clothing; She shall rejoice in time to come. She opens her mouth with wisdom, and on her tongue is the law of kindness.

She watches over the ways of her household, and does not eat the bread of idleness. Her children rise up and call her blessed; Her husband also, and he praises her: "Many daughters have done well, but you excel them all." Charm is deceitful and beauty is passing, but a woman who fears the Lord, she shall be praised. Give her of the fruit of her hands, and let her own works praise her in the gates."

I want to be like this woman when I grow up, how about you? Of all the women we could emulate the Bible gives us a universal example. No matter where you're from, where you live or what you believe this woman is the type of woman we all want to be.

If her children rise and call her blessed now, you can guarantee they will visit her when she's eighty. She married an important man who is known in the city gates and he praises her. She does him good and not evil, so he is likely to be by her side at eighty. She is smart and savvy; she invests and runs a business.

She provides for her household, her children are clothed in scarlet. And she takes care of herself strengthening her arms and being arrayed in fine linen and purple. She is giving and kind to the poor and fears God.

Who wouldn't look up to this woman as a great role model. We can clearly see the choices she's made and the results of her choices. She chooses to rise before dawn and provide food for her house. She chooses to work late into the evening. She chooses to do good to her husband and love her children and they praise her. She chooses to work hard and invest so her family has no lack of gain.

She's not perfect because no one is, but she did the work and made the choices that have us remembering her legacy and desiring to reproduce it. And we don't have to do everything she did to embody her heart and character and reap her rewards.

Maybe you don't want to run a business; you don't have to. But you can see the kinds of choices that need to be made each day to live a life your eighty year old self would be proud to remember.

Google defines virtuous as, "Having or showing high moral standards; especially of a woman." When you choose a new role model such as the woman of Proverbs 31 you are choosing a role model of high moral standards, who can guide you and show you the results of following her lead.

Not all choices are always clear but this one seems pretty cut and dry. You can choose to follow after the role models our culture offers or you can choose a new one. In order to style your soul you have to choose.

You'll have to choose grace over perfection, satisfaction over striving and faith over fear. What will you choose?

Questions

1. What plans did you have for your life when you were younger?

2. What is your vision for your life now?

3. What is your vision for your life when you're eighty?

4. What aspects of the Virtuous woman would you like to imitate?

5. What choices can you make today to make your vision a reality?

Chapter 2

Walking By Faith

Have you ever believed in something that you hadn't personally seen? I've never seen the Eiffel tower with my own eyes but I believe it is in Paris. Why? Well, reputable sources have been to Paris and confirmed its existence; it's been documented in many publications, videos and over time.

Living by faith is very similar. 2 Corinthians 5:7 says, "For we walk by faith, not by sight." We don't have to physically see God to know that He exists and follow His instructions. The same way I trust the sources that have seen the Eiffel tower is the same we can trust the words found in scripture.

If you trust the source, God, you can trust the book, believe and obey. But how can you know that you can trust God? Everyone is known and regarded by their actions. We can read how God interacted with, made promises to and protected those in scripture to see if He is trustworthy.

Does He do what He said He'd do or follow through on His promises? That is the way we measure each other's reliability and trustworthiness.

God told Noah in Genesis six that He was going to destroy the earth with a flood but He would save Noah and anyone in the ark. Did He? Genesis 6:7-8 says, "So the Lord said, "I will destroy man whom I have created from the face of the earth, both man and beast, creeping thing and birds of the air, for I am sorry that I have made them." But Noah found grace in the eyes of the Lord."

Then in Genesis 7:13, 16, 23, 24 we read, "On the very same day Noah and Noah's sons, Shem, Ham, and Japheth, and Noah's wife and the three wives of his sons with them, entered the ark— So those that entered, male and female of all flesh, went in as God had commanded him; and the Lord shut him in. So He destroyed all living things which were on the face of the ground: both man and cattle, creeping thing and bird of the air. They were destroyed from the earth. Only Noah and those who were with him in the ark remained alive. And the waters prevailed on the earth one hundred and fifty days."

God told Abraham that he and his wife Sarah would have a baby, even though Sarah was barren and Abraham was 100 years old. Genesis 17:15-17 says, "Then God said to Abraham, "As for Sarai your wife, you shall not call her name Sarai, but Sarah shall be her name. And I will bless her and also give you a son by her; then I will bless her, and she shall be a mother of nations; kings of peoples shall be from her." Then Abraham fell on his face and laughed, and said in his heart, "Shall a child be born to a man who is one hundred years old? And shall Sarah, who is ninety years old, bear a child?"

And in Genesis 21:1-3 we read, "And the Lord visited Sarah as He had said, and the Lord did for Sarah as He had spoken. For Sarah conceived and bore Abraham a son in his old age, at the set time of which God had spoken to him. And Abraham called the name of his son who was born to him—whom Sarah bore to him—Isaac."

In Exodus God told Moses that He would use him to deliver the children of Israel from Egyptian bondage. In Exodus 3:10 it says, "Come now, therefore, and I will send you to Pharaoh that you may bring My people, the children of Israel, out of Egypt."

And in Exodus 12:31-32 after ten plagues on Egypt it says, "Then he (Pharaoh) called for Moses and Aaron by night, and said, "Rise, go out from among my people, both you and the children of Israel. And go, serve the Lord as you have said. Also take your flocks and your herds, as you have said, and be gone; and bless me also."

In order to do anything by faith we have to believe the source. We wouldn't trust a friend who is perpetually late to take us to an important meeting or event. If we knew someone to be a thief we wouldn't ask them to house sit for us and if we knew a person to be a habitual liar we wouldn't simply take their word on a subject.

Putting your faith in something or someone should be done with great care. We're always encouraged to read the fine print and not to sign legal documents without first reading them all the way through.

So it's imperative that we don't put our faith in just any thing or story, spiritual or otherwise. I read a tragic story once that went like this, "In April 1988 the evening news reported on a photographer who was a skydiver. He had jumped from a plane along with numerous other skydivers and filmed the group as they fell and opened their parachutes.

On the film shown on the telecast, as the final skydiver opened his chute, the picture went berserk. The announcer reported that the cameraman had fallen to his death, having jumped out of the plane without his parachute. It wasn't until he reached for the absent ripcord that he realized he was free falling without a parachute. Until that point, the jump probably seemed exciting and fun. But tragically, he had acted with thoughtless haste and deadly foolishness. Nothing could save him, for his faith was in a parachute never buckled on. Faith in anything but an all-sufficient God can be just as tragic spiritually. Only with faith in Jesus Christ dare we step into the dangerous excitement of life."

Style Your Faith

One of the great things about faith is that no one is born with a certain amount. We all have the ability to strengthen our faith. In fact the Bible tells us to grow in grace. No matter where you find yourself on your faith walk and no matter how you've been tested, you can fashion your faith.

And it's actually through trials and tests that our faith is made stronger. Each time we endure and fight through an obstacle our faith grows. In 2 Kings 5 the Bible speaks of a man named Naaman a great commander in the Syrian army.

Unfortunately Naaman had leprosy, a deadly flesh eating disease, and no way to be healed. Naaman met the prophet Elisha, followed God's instructions to dip in the Jordan river seven times, and was cleansed.

At the end of this trying time in his life Naaman had this to say in 2 Kings 5:15, "And he returned to the man of God, he and all his aides, and came and stood before him; and he said, "Indeed, now I know that there is no God in all the earth, except in Israel..."

Naaman's faith increased after his trial and now he knows that there is but one God. James 1:2-3 tells us to, "Count it all joy, my brothers, when you meet trials of various kinds, for you know that the testing of your faith produces steadfastness."

Steadfastness means, "Firm in purpose, resolution, faith; unwavering, as resolution, faith, adherence, etc... firmly fixed in place or position."

As your faith grows so will your ability to ward off those that would drain your energy with negativity and question your standards. And you will be able to stand for truth. And it will take a lot of faith for us to stay firmly fixed, resolute and trusting.

Plant The Seed

Now that we know we can shape our faith and style it into a mighty force, the question remains how? We discussed growing through trials, but that isn't the only way to increase your faith.

Like all things it takes baby steps and daily action to make something grow big and strong. In order to get to know God we need to get into His word. The only way we can learn the mind of someone is if they tell us, and it's the same with God.

In His infinite love, grace and mercy He didn't hide Himself from us and make us try to guess who He is and what He desires of us; He told us. And reading scripture is the easiest first step to take in growing our faith.

There are many ways to do this and my suggestion is just to start at the beginning. With Bible apps, the internet and good old fashioned books there's no excuse not to start. You don't have to know everything or anything. You only need a willing heart and open mind.

We've all heard the phrase that practice makes perfect and it's true also when growing your faith. Walking your talk is so important. Once you begin to change your thoughts about things your actions will inevitably change as well. And you'll need to practice sticking to your goals and standards when it seems easy to slip back into old ways and thoughts.

There will be easy days and then there will be days when life will seem to come at you from all sides, but those are the days to stick to what you know for sure.

Another great way to grow you faith is to pray. 1 Thessalonians tells us to pray without ceasing and to be anxious for nothing but in prayer to make our requests known to God.

Prayer is a game changer when done effectively. James tells us not to ask for anything with doubts in our minds. Matthew tells us to pray in private and not to have others see us. And in Matthew 6 the disciples ask Jesus to teach them to pray. What many refer to as the Lord's prayer is actually Jesus teaching his apostles how to pray.

Matthew 6:5-15 says, "And when you pray, you shall not be like the hypocrites. For they love to pray standing in the synagogues and on the corners of the streets, that they may be seen by men. Assuredly, I say to you, they have their reward. But you, when you pray, go into your room, and when you have shut your door, pray to your Father who is in the secret place; and your Father who sees in secret will reward you openly. And when you pray, do not use vain repetitions as the heathen do. For they think that they will be heard for their many words.

Therefore do not be like them. For your Father knows the things you have need of before you ask Him. In this manner, therefore, pray: Our Father in heaven, Hallowed be Your name. Your kingdom come. Your will be done On earth as it is in heaven. Give us this day our daily bread. And forgive us our debts, As we forgive our debtors. And do not lead us into temptation, But deliver us from the evil one. For Yours is the kingdom and the power and the glory forever. Amen.

For if you forgive men their trespasses, your heavenly Father will also forgive you. But if you do not forgive men their trespasses, neither will your Father forgive your trespasses."

If you're just starting to pray or you've been praying but feel like maybe your prayers could be more thought out this is a great prayer to model. You can write your prayers out and keep a list of those in need of prayer. Even keeping a prayer journal can be a great help to make sure your prayers don't become rote.

Whenever we learn things it's important to use all five senses to help us remember the information. You can read the scriptures aloud, listen to them on disc or online and an even better way to remember is to write the word.

All you need is a notebook. You can write the entire Bible or you can write out key verses that stick with you as you study. You can also use your notebook to write down definitions of words you may not know and illustrate ideas.

It's your notebook feel free to be as creative as you like and make it fun. Walking by faith is not meant to be a burden or drudgery. Matthew 11:28-30 says, "Come to Me, all you who labor and are heavy laden, and I will give you rest. Take My yoke upon you and learn from Me, for I am gentle and lowly in heart, and you will find rest for your souls. For My yoke is easy and My burden is light."

When you walk by faith not only can you know God and trust Him

Questions

1. Do you trust in God? Why or why not?

2. What are some examples from scripture that show God keeps His word?

3. What are some things you believe in, but have never personally seen?

4. What are some ways to fashion your faith?

Chapter 3

Your Spiritual Wardrobe

You are made of two parts, your physical body and your heavenly spirit. We'll dive more into that in the next chapter, but the same way we dress our physical body we need to dress our spiritual soul.

I love clothes. If I were given a choice between a new outfit, a new handbag or new shoes, I am almost always choosing the outfit. Your spiritual self needs spiritual clothes. And every good wardrobe has some of the same pieces because they are essential and timeless items.

If you were to Google the seven key items every wardrobe needs, not including shoes and accessories, the list would likely include a black dress, a white dress, a colored blouse, jeans, an A-line skirt, trench coat and a blazer.

The seven essential items every spiritual wardrobe needs can be found in 2 Peter 1:5-8 which says, "But also for this very reason, giving all diligence, add to your faith virtue, to virtue knowledge, to knowledge self-control, to self-control perseverance, to perseverance godliness, to godliness brotherly kindness, and to brotherly kindness love. For if these things are yours and abound, you will be neither barren nor unfruitful in the knowledge of our Lord Jesus Christ."

Let's take a look at each of these and find out how to add them to our spiritual closet so that our inner person is just as beautiful as our physical person.

Virtue

We discussed the definition of virtue earlier as having high morals. Webster's dictionary added, "Conformity to a standard of right: morality b: a particular moral excellence." We then looked at the woman of Proverbs 31 and her character and life choices that granted her the title of virtuous woman.

But there is another woman in scripture who was said to be known as a virtuous woman. That woman is Ruth. As the book opens we find Ruth a widow, being sent back to her homeland and about to face separation from her mother-in-law. Ruth chooses not to return to her homeland but instead follows and cares for Naomi, her mother-in-law.

Ruth and Naomi return to Naomi's homeland and are immediately faced with trials of being poor and destitute with no protection from family. Naomi encourages Ruth to go and work in a relative's field to gather food for them and she does.

She works tirelessly and when the relative, Boaz, notices her and makes provisions for and invites her to lunch she joins him and saves some food for Naomi. When he encourages her not to work in anyone else's field she listens and obeys.

Naomi then seeks to have Ruth married to Boaz, as is their tradition and Ruth does all that Naomi says. We'll join the story here in Ruth 3:5-10 which says, "And she said to her, "All that you say to me I will do." So she went down to the threshing floor and did according to all that her mother-in-law instructed her. And after Boaz had eaten and drunk, and his heart was cheerful, he went to lie down at the end of the heap of grain; and she came softly, uncovered his feet, and lay down.

Now it happened at midnight that the man was startled, and turned himself; and there, a woman was lying at his feet. And he said, "Who are you?" So she answered, "I am Ruth, your maidservant. Take your maidservant under your wing, for you are a close relative."

Then he said, "Blessed are you of the Lord, my daughter! For you have shown more kindness at the end than at the beginning, in that you did not go after young men, whether poor or rich. And now, my daughter, do not fear. I will do for you all that you request, for all the people of my town know that you are a virtuous woman."

How did all of the people know Ruth was a virtuous woman? Because of the choices she made, her character, her care for her mother-in-law and her manner of life."

If we are to add virtue to our spiritual closet as the basis for everything else you can see how important it is to have standards and keep to them. Webster defines morality as, "A doctrine or system of moral conduct."

The Bible is often called doctrine or the gospel. It's God's system of how we are to behave and defines what is right and what is wrong. And before you can add anything else to your faith or your spiritual outfit you have to have this belief firmly in place.

I know our culture wants us to believe that we decide what's right and wrong based on our situation, but God says there is always right and wrong no matter the situation. It's these truths that you must search out, believe wholeheartedly and obey.

Knowledge

2 Peter next tells us to add knowledge to virtue. Once we firmly have our morals and virtue in place we need to seek Jesus. Philippians 2:1-5 tells us to have the same mind as Jesus. It says, "Therefore if there is any consolation in Christ, if any comfort of love, if any fellowship of the Spirit, if any affection and mercy, fulfill my joy by being like-minded, having the same

love, being of one accord, of one mind. Let nothing be done through selfish ambition or conceit, but in lowliness of mind let each esteem others better than himself. Let each of you look out not only for his own interests, but also for the interests of others. Let this mind be in you which was also in Christ Jesus."

The only way to know something is to study it. We all have heard the phrase, "Knowledge is power." And we all know it to be incredibly true. Do you remember not knowing something? Do you remember learning it? How did you feel after?

Without knowledge we can easily be deceived, led astray or simply go the wrong way. Knowledge is key to understanding the world around you. How can you effectively complete an assignment for school if you don't know the topic, how long should it be or when it is due? How can you work for a company if you don't know what is required of you?

How much more important is it to learn what God wants for your life? There are many people who stand at the ready to tell you their version of what God wants for you and it usually involves giving money to them.

But why trust another person when you can know for yourself? You have everything you need to learn God and know the path to happiness, joy, fulfillment and salvation.

The entire book of Proverbs is a book of knowledge. Proverbs 1:2-4 tell us why the book was written. It says, "To know wisdom and instruction, to perceive the words of understanding, to receive the instruction of wisdom, justice, judgment, and equity; to give prudence to the simple, to the young man knowledge and discretion."

If you want to add knowledge to your spiritual closet start in Proverbs. Proverbs 1:7 says, "The fear of the Lord is the beginning of knowledge, but fools despise wisdom and instruction."

Self Control

The next key item in our wardrobe is self control. Have you ever lost control, maybe in anger? Have you ever felt out of control, maybe with food? Self control is a beautiful thing because the Bible doesn't put it in the hands of others. You get to control you and I get to control me. Too much for you may not be enough for me and vice versa.

I have a sweet tooth that needs constant monitoring. Chocolate chip cookies are my favorite, but they are not my teeth and stomach's favorite when I eat an entire package. Proverbs 24:16 would admonish me with these words, "Have you found honey? Eat only as much as you need, lest you be filled with it and vomit."

However, self control is no easy feat. In a culture that encourages excess and tells you to treat yourself and that you deserve it; it can be hard to tell yourself no. Sometimes in an effort to constrain yourself you have to get angry.

For me I grew angry and tired of feeling sick and sluggish each time I indulged in some sweet treat to excess. I had to ask was the temporary delight worth the constant pain and suffering that I was inflicting on myself?

I don't know what area you struggle to control yourself in but I do know you'll have to choose. You'll have to choose yourself over the thing that is taxing you.

Moses chose to leave Egypt; even though he was a prince there and instead become a shepherd in the desert and later returned to free his people.

Hebrews 11:24-26 says, "By faith Moses, when he became of age, refused to be called the son of Pharaoh's daughter, choosing rather to suffer affliction with the people of God than to enjoy the passing pleasures of sin, esteeming the reproach of Christ greater riches than the treasures in Egypt; for he looked to the reward."

Help Yourself

One of the best ways I've found to control yourself, your emotions, your words and your feelings is simply to keep silent and wait. Wait it out. Allow ten minutes to pass before giving yourself permission to give in. You'll probably notice like I do that the desire or impulse will vanish.

Another way to strengthen your self control is to implement systems. If you struggle with money, leave your credit card at home or move to a cash only system. Systems are wonderful because once they are in place you no longer have to think about them and when you have the desire to put something on your credit card you won't be able.

I once saw a woman freeze her credit card in a block of ice, maybe that will prevent online shopping as well. Do whatever you need to do to help yourself.

Hebrews 12:11 says, "Now no chastening (discipline) seems to be joyful for the present, but painful; nevertheless, afterward it yields the peaceable fruit of righteousness to those who have been trained by it."

We have to train ourselves or rather re-train ourselves to love self control and not give in to the belief that it somehow limits us or takes something from us; when it in fact strengthens us.

Perseverance

Perseverance is defined as, "Steadfastness in doing something despite difficulty or delay in achieving success."

I recently spoke at a ladies retreat and the theme was women of war. I spoke about the spiritual war we're in and how to win it. And as I wrote that lesson I was constantly reminded of a soldier's dedication and perseverance. And I thought to apply it to my own life as I raise my children, live as an obedient wife and fight the good fight.

And the more I thought about it the more I began to feel that my commitment was not in question but my consistency and determination.

Galatians 6:9 says, "And let us not grow weary while doing good, for in due season we shall reap if we do not lose heart."

Which is why I believe we must relent less and persevere. We cannot lose heart, grow tired or give up. The stakes are too high and our enemy never does. He truly is relentless in his pursuit of our souls and the souls of our family and friends.

Perseverance in any area is tough; maintaining that burning fire in your heart isn't always easy but when it is done the benefits and the results are immeasurable.

Paul says in Philippians 3:12-14 says, "Not that I have already attained, or am already perfected; but I press on, that I may lay hold of that for which Christ Jesus has also laid hold of me. Brethren, I do not count myself to have apprehended; but one thing I do, forgetting those things which are behind and reaching forward to those things which are ahead, I press toward the goal for the prize of the upward call of God in Christ Jesus."

Like Paul we can't run forward if we're constantly looking back. The past is done and we can't go back. The present is now and the future hasn't happened yet. We have to continue to press on even when the road gets hard, when we get weak and when others try to tear us down.

Keep your eyes on the prize at all times and trust God to see you through any obstacle.

Godliness

Next we are told to add godliness to our spiritual wardrobe. Dictionary.com says godliness is, "Conforming to the laws and wishes of God; devout; pious, coming from God; divine."

The Bible encourages us on many occasions to be like God. 1 Peter 1:13-16 says, "Therefore gird up the loins of your mind, be sober, and rest your hope fully upon the grace that is to be brought to you at the revelation of Jesus Christ; as obedient children, not conforming yourselves to the former lusts, as in your ignorance; but as He who called you is holy, you also be holy in all your conduct, because it is written, "Be holy, for I am holy."

Webster's say holy is, "Devoted entirely to God or the work of God a: having a divine quality b: venerated as or as if sacred."

Romans 12:1-2 says, "I beseech you therefore, brethren, by the mercies of God, that you present your bodies a living sacrifice, holy, acceptable to God, which is your reasonable service. And do not be conformed to this world, but be transformed by the renewing of your mind, that you may prove what is that good and acceptable and perfect will of God."

And 1 Timothy 6:6 says, "Now godliness with contentment is great gain." Living a holy and devout life before God is great gain. In Bible times they knew Jesus' disciples by the way they lived and the things they said.

Acts 4:13 says, "Now when they saw the boldness of Peter and John, and perceived that they were uneducated and untrained men, they marveled. And they realized that they had been with Jesus." They saw Peter and John's boldness, heard the words they said in the previous verses and realized they'd been with Jesus.

When we add godliness to our faith we want people to be able to look at us and know we've been with Jesus.

Brotherly Kindness

Girls and women get a bad rap as gossips, back biters and for being catty. But when you style your soul in all of these virtues brotherly kindness is a way of life.

Brotherly kindness is about preferring others, loving your brothers and sisters and being kind to those in the faith with you. It's generally easier to be nice and show kindness to strangers than it is to show kindness to those closest to you.

But that is not to be the case in the sisterhood. Romans 12:10-13 says, "Be kindly affectionate to one another with brotherly love, in honor giving preference to one another; not lagging in diligence, fervent in spirit, serving the Lord; rejoicing in hope, patient in tribulation, continuing steadfastly in prayer; distributing to the needs of the saints, given to hospitality."

I remember a story I heard once in a sermon that went like this, "Two boys were arguing over a toy. The older brother told the younger to let him play with it and the younger told the older it was his turn to play with it. Their mother heard them fighting and when she entered the room she asked, "What would Jesus do?" Almost in unison they replied he would let the other play with the toy. Their mother smiled and left the room. The younger brother turned to the older brother and said, "You be Jesus, okay."

Adding brotherly kindness to our wardrobe turns us all into Jesus. We look out for one another, care for and protect one another. I love the quote that says, "Be kind to everyone, for we are all fighting a battle."

And isn't it true? We all have our personal struggles and some days are harder than others. We need to hear kind words and be offered good deeds and affection, especially by those who also profess to love Jesus.

Galatians 6:10 says, "Therefore, as we have opportunity, let us do good to all, especially to those who are of the household of faith."

Love

Love is such a small but mighty word. The Bible says love covers a multitude of sins. It tells us love is the reason God sent Jesus to die on the cross for us and if we get nothing else get love.

Our culture loves love; but they are enraptured by a perversion of love. Love is not agreeing with everything someone says or does. Love doesn't make allowances for your wrong doing, and love certainly isn't simply "not judging."

Love isn't forced, bred from fear or coerced. So what is love and how can you show it? 1 Corinthians 13 tells us exactly what love does, how it acts, reacts and shows itself.

1 Corinthians 13:1-8 says, "Though I speak with the tongues of men and of angels, but have not love, I have become sounding brass or a clanging

cymbal. And though I have the gift of prophecy, and understand all mysteries and all knowledge, and though I have all faith, so that I could remove mountains, but have not love, I am nothing. And though I bestow all my goods to feed the poor, and though I give my body to be burned, but have not love, it profits me nothing. Love suffers long and is kind; love does not envy; love does not parade itself, is not puffed up; does not behave rudely, does not seek its own, is not provoked, thinks no evil; does not rejoice in iniquity, but rejoices in the truth; bears all things, believes all things, hopes all things, endures all things. Love never fails... And now abide faith, hope, love, these three; but the greatest of these is love."

Who do you love? We love our parents, spouses, children and some special friends. And even though we use the term loosely, earlier I said I love clothes, I'm very fond of clothes but I don't actually love them.

Love isn't always very complicated we can easily tell when someone loves us and when we have built a relationship with someone based on mutual trust, understanding and faith. The Bible discusses four types of love in scripture, agape (is the kind of love God has for us), phileo (brotherly love), eros (romantic love) and storge (family love).

Each kind of love is important when reading and learning God's word. Love is very active as you read in 1 Corinthians 13; it seeks the other person's good and controls itself. It's humble and giving and it never fails.

You can't go wrong siding with love. It'll help you overcome obstacles and obstinate people. Proverbs 25:21-22 says, "If your enemy is hungry, give him bread to eat; and if he is thirsty, give him water to drink; for so you will heap coals of fire on his head, and the Lord will reward you."

We began in 2 Peter 1 with our list of seven essential pieces every spiritual wardrobe needs. Verse 8 of the chapter says, "For if these things are yours and abound, you will be neither barren nor unfruitful in the knowledge of our Lord Jesus Christ."

Questions

1. What are the seven items every spiritual wardrobe needs?

2. What are some things you didn't know but are glad you know now?

3. What are some areas of self control that you need to improve? How?

4. What does it mean to be holy? Are you holy?

Part 2

Walking Worthy

Chapter 4

Who Am I?

A popular idea today is to find your true self. Figuring out who you are and why you are on this earth is an important task. Mark Twain said, "The two most important days in your life are the day you are born and the day you find out why." This is going to sound presumptuous but I am going to answer those questions for you. I know you want to know how I could know who you are, especially considering the fact that some of us have never met. But consider this, 2. Tim. 3:16-17 says, "All Scripture is given by inspiration of God, and is profitable for doctrine, for reproof, for correction, for instruction in righteousness, that the man of God may be complete, thoroughly equipped for every good work." So let's search the scriptures together and figure out how I know the answers to these questions.

Eccl. 12:13 says, "Let us hear the conclusion of the whole matter: fear God and keep His commandments for this is man's all." We are on this earth to serve God; that is probably not news to you but let's also look at Rom. 1:9 which says, "For God is my witness, whom I serve with my spirit in the gospel of His Son, that without ceasing I make mention of you always in my prayers." We're on this earth to serve God and Paul says that he serves God with his spirit as opposed to serving in the flesh.

You are made in the image of God, (Gen. 1:26). John 4:24 is the verse we used to learn how to worship. Remember it says, "God is Spirit, and those who worship Him must worship in spirit and truth." You are a soul in a body, not a body housing a soul. Your soul is who you are; your soul is your very being. Adam when he was created was not a living being until God breathed into him the breath of life or breathed into him his soul. Once we realize and accept this it's a very freeing sensation. No longer have we any need to be concerned with the things of this world; it truly epitomizes what is meant when we sing the song this world is not our home. But knowing is only half the battle.

1 Pet. 2:11 says, "Beloved, I beg you as sojourners and pilgrims, abstain from fleshly lusts which war against the soul." Stop fighting your true self. Peter says we're sojourners and pilgrims. We won't be here forever and giving into fleshly lusts is only hurting us. This is most encouraging since your soul is who you are, your body cannot do anything without you giving into it. Have you ever heard of anything tempting your soul? They are called fleshly lusts for a reason. What on this earth could possibly tempt your soul? Nothing, temptation is only for the body. Our culture tempts us not so much directly but with ideas. Ideas that we are less than someone else or not good enough. Ideas that who we are is made up of things outside of us; it's not true, but unfortunately some of us are believing it.

There is a car commercial that takes a professional male or female athlete, shows them in their uniform and then strips them down to their underwear. They then proceed to dress them up in evening clothes, a dress for a woman or business suit for a man. The tagline to the commercial says aggression in its most elegant form. This is the very definition of temptation; it's the lure of sin in its most elegant form. It's fornication, lasciviousness and lust wrapped up in a love story, it's theft and deception wrapped up in an action underdog story and it's murder wrapped up in a women's rights movement. If sin showed you its true self your soul, your true self, would immediately be repulsed and reject it, but sin doesn't immediately show you its true colors. 2. Cor. 11:14-15 says, "And no wonder! For Satan himself transforms himself into an angel of light. Therefore it is no great thing if his ministers also transform themselves into ministers of righteousness, whose end will be according to their works."

You have to take back control of your life. You have to decide today to serve God with your spirit like Paul stated in Rom. 1:9. And the only way to do that is to feed and treat your true self the way you feed and treat the body that houses it.

2. Cor. 4:16-18 says, "Therefore we do not lose heart. Even though our outward man is perishing, yet the inward man is being renewed day by day. For our light affliction, which is but for a moment, is working for us a far more exceeding and eternal weight of glory, while we do not look at the things which are seen, but at the things which are not seen. For the things which are seen are temporary, but the things which are not seen are eternal." We must expand our minds ladies to see the things which are not seen, to live in that arena. We have to know and accept that our true selves are only here for a short while and we cannot spend the time that we have on insecurity, jealousy and living for this life.

Think about those five wise and five foolish virgins of Matt. 25. The wise virgins prepared themselves for their eternal home. What if, when this life is over, we're transformed and given new bodies but the new bodies appear the way our souls were provided for on earth? Would we have malnourished souls while our bodies, which are now dead, were kept in pristine condition, heaven forbid! Rom. 12:1-2 says, "I beseech you therefore, brethren, by the mercies of God, that you present your bodies a living sacrifice, holy, acceptable to God, which is your reasonable service. And do not be conformed to this world, but be transformed by the renewing of your mind, that you may prove what is that good and acceptable and perfect will of God."

These two verses are why you were put on this earth. May we all free our minds from the binds of worldly thinking and living and put our focus on preparing our true selves for our eternal home.

God's Beauty Standard

Have you ever considered what your soul looks like? Oh we spend countless hours examining what our physical bodies look like but since we now know that our true selves are our souls and that God doesn't look on the outward appearance; we should make sure that our souls are presentable to the Lord. But you can't apply physical makeup to your soul, right? How can you make up your soul? You have to first decide whose standard of beauty you'll follow.

Long lashes, pouty lips, defined eyes and rosy cheeks are where the world would have you believe your beauty is contained. Take a look at any fashion magazine, billboard or television show. Advertisements and articles are telling you that you should aspire to look like girls and women who have been digitally buffed, air brushed and elongated. Not only are you told to try and emulate these computer generated images; you are then told to look like them forever. Age defying, wrinkle and puffiness reducing serums are then brought into the mix so that we can be forever young. Take it from someone who spent most of their teen years studying Allure magazine and personally testing any and all serums, creams and eye enhancing shades; imitation is not possible. You will never be able to look like the Photoshop model du jour; and why try? God only created one of you there is no need for comparisons.

Many of us spend too much time concerned about our perceived inferiority and not enough time glorying in our worth as a creature made in the image of God. Gen. 1:26 says, "And God said, Let us make man in Our image, after Our likeness: and let them have dominion over the fish of the sea, and over the fowl of the air, and over the cattle, and over all the earth, and over every creeping thing that creeps upon the earth." Psalm 8:3-5 says, "When I consider Your heavens, the work of Your fingers, The moon and the stars, which You have ordained, what is man that You are mindful of him, and the son of man that You visit him? For You have made him a little lower than the angels, and You have crowned him with glory and honor."

God thought so much of you that He made you in His image and crowned you with glory and honor. There's no need to desire and try to become Ms. America, fight over an earthly crown and have someone else decide whether or not you're beautiful enough. You already have an eternal crown given to you by a loving and eternal God.

Have you ever noticed how people assume that the children of celebrities will look like them? Then when the children are born they don't look anything like their parents. Not so with Christians, our Father is beautiful and has made us in His image. Psalm 27:4 says, "One thing I have desired of the LORD, that will I seek: that I may dwell in the house of the LORD all the days of my life, to behold the beauty of the LORD, and to inquire in His temple." Have you ever considered the fact that God is beautiful? While the Bible is clear that no man has ever seen God, (John 1:18), perhaps His beauty manifests itself in a different way. If we can figure out how God shows His beauty and we are made in His image we ought to be able to show the same kind of beauty.

The word beauty is defined by Webster's Dictionary as, "The quality present in a thing or person that gives intense pleasure or deep satisfaction to the mind, whether arising from sensory manifestations (as shape, color, sound, etc.), a meaningful design or pattern, or something else (as a personality in which high spiritual qualities are manifest)."

So no one has seen the Lord yet Psalm 27:4 says He is beautiful and Webster's Dictionary says one definition of beauty is a personality in which high spiritual qualities are manifest. Aha I say! God has to be the most beautiful Being because He has the highest spiritual qualities. The question now is whose standard of beauty are we attempting to emulate?

The world and mass media would have us believe that only tall, thin, leggy, long haired and tanned women are beautiful, and if you don't fit into this extra small box then there is something wrong with you. Au contraire my friend, maybe if we take a step back from the looking glass we could clearly see that it is not we who are striving for the wrong definition of beauty but them. The latter part of 1. Sam. 16:7 says, "For the LORD does not see as man sees; for man looks at the outward appearance, but the LORD looks at the heart." I. Pet. 3:3-4 says, "Do not let your adornment be merely outward arranging the hair, wearing gold, or putting on fine apparel rather let it be the hidden person of the heart, with the incorruptible beauty of a gentle and quiet spirit, which is very precious in the sight of God."

There it is God's standard of beauty. The verses say that God's beauty standard will grant you incorruptible beauty. Webster defines incorruptible as, "That will not dissolve, disintegrate, decay, etc." This means if we emulate God's standard of beauty we will be beautiful forever without the use of Botox or other plastic surgeries.

So decide, do you want to be beautiful forever and follow God's standard because it doesn't matter what we look like on the outside everyone can be beautiful like the Lord. With God as our example of beauty we could all walk around with paper bags on our heads and still be beautiful. But any beauty expert worth their salt will tell you that you need the right tools to obtain the look. What tools do we need to be beautiful like God? Every look starts with a good base.

Foundation

Traditional foundation is used to mask or hide imperfections. If you find the right shade it will work brilliantly and you will have flawless skin; that is until you wash your face at night. Once the foundation is removed you can clearly see your imperfections again. It's not so with God's foundation. God's foundation is healing. It has the ability to remove imperfections permanently. You have no need for concealer with God's foundation. It isn't based on oils and powders; God's foundation is based on love.

The same way expectant parents prepare a nursery before the baby is born. The Godhead prepared the world for us and on the sixth day created man to enjoy it. After man and woman sinned by eating of the fruit of the tree of knowledge of good and evil, God went back to work to restore us to Him.

We read Acts 7 in a previous chapter and saw how God's plan unfolded. He sent Jesus, His only son, to die for us on the cruel cross of Calvary so that we might be able to have a home with Him in heaven. Rom. 5:8 says, "But God demonstrates His own love toward us, in that while we were still sinners, Christ died for us."

Before Jesus came there was no way to permanently remove sins. Heb. 10:1-4 says, "For the law, having a shadow of the good things to come, and not the very image of the things, can never with these same sacrifices, which they offer continually year by year, make those who approach perfect. For then would they not have ceased to be offered? For the worshipers, once purified, would have had no more consciousness of sins. But in those sacrifices there is a reminder of sins every year. For it is not possible that the blood of bulls and goats could take away sins."

Later in that same chapter verses 12 and 18 say of Christ, "But this Man, after He had offered one sacrifice for sins forever, sat down at the right hand of God." "Now where there is remission of these, there is no longer an offering for sin." Jesus walked this very earth teaching and preaching the kingdom of God. He laid down His life so that our souls could be taken up to heaven after death. 2. Pet. 3:9 says, "The Lord is not slack concerning His promise, as some count slackness, but is longsuffering toward us, not willing that any should perish but that all should come to repentance."

Salvation through Jesus has nothing to do with sinner's prayers or boxes to sit in and make confessions. In order to stand flawless before the Lord you must obey His word. If you want your imperfections and the guilt associated with them removed, faith with obedience is necessary. Sounds exactly like our reason for worshipping. The Bible is all encompassing and has the answers for every aspect of our lives.

The first thing we must do is hear the gospel preached, Rom. 10:17 says, "Faith comes by hearing and hearing by the word of God." It's Noah being told in Gen. 6 to build an ark, he heard the word of God. Next you have to believe. Mark 15:16 says, "He who believes and is baptized will be saved;

but he who does not believe will be condemned."

Back to Noah, he believed the word of God and therefore obeyed it and built the ark. After you believe you must repent of sins, Romans 3:23 says all have sinned and Acts 2:38 says, "Then Peter said to them, "Repent, and let every one of you be baptized in the name of Jesus Christ for the remission of sins; and you shall receive the gift of the Holy Spirit." Once you've repented you need to confess the name of Jesus, Acts 8:36-37 says, "Now as they went down the road, they came to some water. And the eunuch said, "See, here is water. What hinders me from being baptized?" Then Philip said, "If you believe with all your heart, you may." And he answered and said, "I believe that Jesus Christ is the Son of God." As you can see from the last three verses mentioned baptism is an integral part of salvation and so we must all be baptized in order to be saved as it says in John 3:5, "Jesus answered, "Most assuredly, I say to you, unless one is born of water and the Spirit, he cannot enter the kingdom of God." Once you're baptized you need only remain faithful and heaven is yours.

This is God's foundation; loving us so much He gave His only Son to die for us when we least deserved it. His foundation has the power to cleanse you of scars left behind by sins against yourself and others. God's foundation of love is the base for the rest of your look. You can't emulate God's beauty without it. Love makes everyone look and feel beautiful. 1. Pet. 4:8 says, "And above all things have fervent love for one another, for "love will cover a multitude of sins."

Once we put on God's foundation we can practice having gentle and quiet spirits by meditating on the word, using our talents in service for the Lord and letting our lights shine. Being kind to yourself and others are also great ways to display your gentle spirit. Take Esther for example. Esther was taken with a large number of women as a candidate to be queen, and was chosen. When you read the second chapter of the book of Esther it says nothing of her physical beauty. We don't know if she had blue or brown eyes, a large or small nose, long or short hair. What the verses do give us is a glimpse at the spirit of

Esther.

Esther 2:15-17 says, "Now when the turn came for Esther the daughter of Abihail the uncle of Mordecai, who had taken her as his daughter, to go in to the king, she requested nothing but what Hegai the king's eunuch, the custodian of the women, advised. And Esther obtained favor in the sight of all who saw her. So Esther was taken to King Ahasuerus, into his royal palace, in the tenth month, which is the month of Tebeth, in the seventh year of his reign. The king loved Esther more than all the other women, and she obtained grace and favor in his sight more than all the virgins; so he set the royal crown upon her head and made her queen instead of Vashti."

Verse 15 shows us that Esther was able to heed instruction and take advice. It also says she found grace and favor in the king's sight. This doesn't sound like she was talking loudly about all of the things she would do as queen or acting boisterously on her way to see the king. Remember Esther's example and use her as a guide as you apply the foundation for a quiet and gentle spirit.

Blush

Jeremiah 6:13-15 says, "Because from the least of them even to the greatest of them, everyone is given to covetousness; and from the prophet even to the priest, everyone deals falsely. They have also healed the hurt of My people slightly, Saying, 'Peace, peace!' When there is no peace. Were they ashamed when they had committed abomination? No! They were not at all ashamed; nor did they know how to blush. Therefore they shall fall among those who fall; at the time I punish them, they shall be cast down," says the LORD."

Unfortunately this is the state of many girls and women today. They are given to covetousness, commit abominations and have forgotten how to blush. If we were to describe the state of women today based off of what is portrayed in mass media; we'd all need to blush. Women have cast off the idea of being the weaker vessel in their pursuit of equality with men and they have lost all shame.

Girls are on television being wholly disrespectful to their parents while showing off their lavish bedrooms and super sweet sixteen birthday parties. Their mothers are physically and verbally assaulting their so called friends on their own housewives of whatever television show. Women have entire careers based on how many men they've slept with; they have no idea what it means to have a quiet and gentle spirit because it's all about them all of the time. And it's these women that society deems the most beautiful in the world. Are these displays God's plan and desire for women? Have we removed God so far from the equation that now anything goes? If there is no change our looks will be just as effected as our character.

Proverbs 12:4 says, "An excellent wife is the crown of her husband, But she who causes shame is like rottenness in his bones." Gal. 5:19-21 gives us a list of shameful acts that many people today simply overlook. Gal. 5:19-21 says, "Now the works of the flesh are evident, which are: adultery, fornication, uncleanness, lewdness, idolatry, sorcery, hatred, contentions, jealousies, outbursts of wrath, selfish ambitions, dissensions, heresies, envy, murders, drunkenness, revelries, and the like; of which I tell you beforehand, just as I also told you in time past, that those who practice such things will not inherit the kingdom of God."

All of pop culture is made up of these. No one watches the shows and movies or listens to the music unless someone is having an angry outburst, is full of jealousy, going out partying wildly or practicing selfish ambitions. None of these acts when played out in the media are actually beautiful. But that's what every woman wants right, to be seen as beautiful? Yet no one has taken a step back to see that the standard of beauty they're using isn't working.

Blush is used to make cheeks rosy and to give a more youthful appearance. Eccl. 12 says to remember your Creator in the days of youth but many obviously did not. God's blush comes from a sincere heart to learn and obey His word, to be able to set yourself apart for the Lord. God's beauty standard is based on love and having a quiet and gentle spirit. The world's standard is completely opposite. Rom. 1:28-32 gives us yet another list of shameful acts but adds a key piece at the end. Rom. 1:28-32 says, "And even as they did not like to retain God in their knowledge, God gave them over to a debased mind, to do those things which are not fitting; being filled with all unrighteousness, sexual immorality, wickedness, covetousness, maliciousness; full of envy, murder, strife, deceit, evil-mindedness; they are whisperers, backbiters, haters of God, violent, proud, boasters, inventors of evil things, disobedient to parents, undiscerning, untrustworthy, unloving, unforgiving, unmerciful; who, knowing the righteous judgment of God, that those who practice such things are deserving of death, not only do the same but also approve of those who practice them."

I love the Bible for its thoroughness. No one is off the hook. At the end of verse 32 it says that not only the people who do the deeds are worthy of death but also the ones who approve of their deeds. So for people who say that they personally are not homosexual but they don't see anything wrong with it or for those who say they personally don't spread gossip but are quick to listen to it; I say beware. Let us not be named among the girls and women who have lost the ability to blush.

Let us practice discernment and be able to see these actions for what they really are, abominations. Let us not be counted among those who approve of things that the Lord does not.

Eye Liner

We'll finish off our everyday incorruptible look with a bit of eye opening eyeliner. Did you know that if you have large eyes and you want to make them look smaller you use eyeliner to line the top lid and if you have small eyes you want to appear larger you line the bottom lid? That's a beauty tip for our physical bodies, but with God's standard of beauty He opens our eyes in a completely different way.

In Gen. 21 Hagar had just been sent away from the house of Abraham with her son Ishmael. She was tired and thirsty and had hidden her son away from her to perish. But the angel of God came to her and spoke to her and in verses 18-20 He said, "Arise, lift up the lad and hold him with your hand, for I will make him a great nation." Then God opened her eyes, and she saw a well of water. And she went and filled the skin with water, and gave the lad a drink. So God was with the lad; and he grew and dwelt in the wilderness, and became an archer." The word of God is eye opening. He opened Hagar's eyes to see that He had not left her and had indeed provided salvation for her and her baby.

In another instance God opened the eyes of Balaam. In Num. 22 Balaam wanted to go with Balak to curse the Israelites after God had expressly told him no. Balak asked again and Balaam said he would see what more God had to say. As we all know God is perfect, He has no more to say once He gives an answer. The second time he asked God told Balaam to go with Balak and Balaam was met by an Angel of the Lord. Num. 22: 31-32 says, "Then the LORD opened Balaam's eyes, and he saw the Angel of the LORD standing in the way with His drawn sword in His hand; and he bowed his head and fell flat on his face. And the Angel of the LORD said to him, "Why have you struck your donkey these three times? Behold, I have come out to stand against you, because your way is perverse before Me."

God opened Balaam's eyes just in time to see the danger before him that his donkey tried to save him from three times. God's word is also able to open our eyes to His truths and His true standard of beauty. True beauty has nothing to do with using eyeliner to make our eyes larger or smaller but it has to do with having our eyes exercised to discern right from wrong. Heb. 5:14 says, "But solid food belongs to those who are of full age, that is, those who by reason of use have their senses exercised to discern both good and evil."

Let's make sure we've allowed God to open our eyes to the reality of sin. We must exercise our eyes through different experiences and studying to be able to make accurate judgments between what's right and what's wrong.

Now that we know how to apply God's makeup we can have incorruptible beauty. We can have a quiet and gentle spirit, which is precious to God. You can discern between what is good and evil no matter how pop culture tries to spin the actions. Know that no matter if you're having the worst hair day in the history of bad hair days as long as you keep applying God's standard of true beauty to your life you will find grace and favor in the eyes of everyone who sees you.

Questions

1. How do you know that you are a soul in a body not a body housing a soul? Hint: Gen. 2

2. Fleshly lusts war against your soul. What temptations are you constantly battling and how can you overcome them?

3. Where and how does sin hide, so that you don't immediately see its true nature?

4. Whose standard of beauty have you decided to follow?

5. How is God's beauty manifest?

6. Has pop culture desensitized you to sin? Can you still blush?

Chapter 5

Modesty Starts In The Mind

Women who style their souls know that modesty is more than just what we put on, it's what we put in. We know that modesty begins way before we get up and walk to our closets; modesty begins in the mind.

Modesty on Dictionary.com is defined as, "Having or showing regard for the decencies of behavior, speech, dress, c.; decent: a modest neckline on a dress." Generally, when we use the word modest we use it the way the dictionary does to describe the way our clothing fits. However, let's focus on the way the word is used in 1 Tim. 2:9 and 1 Pet. 3:3-5.

1. Tim. 2:9-10 says, "In like manner also, that the women adorn themselves in modest apparel, with propriety and moderation, not with braided hair or gold or pearls or costly clothing, but, which is proper for women professing godliness, with good works." Also, 1 Pet. 3:3-5 says, "Do not let your adornment be merely outward—arranging the hair, wearing gold, or putting on fine apparel—rather let it be the hidden person of the heart, with the incorruptible beauty of a gentle and quiet spirit, which is very precious in the sight of God. For in this manner, in former times, the holy women who trusted in God also adorned themselves, being submissive to their own

husbands."

The word modest used in these verses is the Greek word kosmeeos, which means to be orderly arranged or decorous. The focus in these verses is not so much about women who wear clothes that are tight or low cut. The women in these verses are actually over dressing, and Paul and Peter are telling them that their focus should be on the hidden person of the heart. As we noted in the last chapter true beauty shines from the inside out. In order to focus on our hidden persons, our true selves, we need to guard our minds, renew our minds and change the channel from Me TV to Christ Central.

Guard Your Mind

When focusing on our hearts the first thing we need to do is guard it. Your mind is your spiritual heart. You must guard it because your mind is constantly under attack. Everyone is trying to infiltrate it with their own agendas.

When I was in college I minored in marketing and we spent countless hours discussing the why and how people bought things, why when people enter a store they always go to the right, why they picked one lid over two and so on. The gist of the class was if you can get people to see, desire and think about something; they will buy it. The Bible says it this way in 1 John 2:16, "For all that is in the world—the lust of the flesh, the lust of the eyes, and the pride of life—is not of the Father but is of the world." It's how Satan got Eve in the garden. Gen 3:6 says, "So when the woman saw that the tree was good for food, that it was pleasant to the eyes, and a tree desirable to make one wise, she took of its fruit and ate. She also gave to her husband with her, and he ate."

She saw the fruit, desired it and took it. You must guard your mind because once something gets in it's incredibly hard to get it back out. It's especially hard when the something that gets in is something that you desire. Sometimes it might not be good for you; it's my constant battle with chocolate chip cookies!

We looked at Matt. 15:17-18 earlier and the same scriptures apply here as well. In this passage Jesus says, "Do you not yet understand that whatever enters the mouth goes into the stomach and is eliminated? But those things which proceed out of the mouth come from the heart, and they defile a man." Television, movies, books, music and friends are daily implanting things in your mind. I know some of you may be thinking 'I don't even watch Desperate Housewives so she's not talking to me.' You may not watch it but you might hang out with one, and she is slowly infiltrating your mind to think like her. If she is constantly talking about people in the congregation or her husband; how long before you begin to think and see things her way?

I. Cor. 15:33, says "Do not be deceived: "Evil company corrupts good habits." Did you notice the last part of Genesis 3:6 it said, "She also gave to her husband with her, and he ate." Adam wasn't the one looking at and desiring the tree but Eve's bad decision was enough to influence Adam to join her. Girlfriend do not be deceived whatever you put or let in is going to influence you and eventually come out.

You must also guard your mind because your thoughts determine your actions. Everything you put on your body and the way you act says something about the way you think and the type of person you are. If I were to wear a trench coat to the fourth of July fireworks display what might that say to onlookers? It might say I am trying to hide or sell them something. What are your intentions when you get dressed for school, work or worship, because whatever you put on, you're ensemble is speaking to people for you. Your dress might not be as severe as that last example but do you wear things knowing you shouldn't?

I have spent quite a deal of time in my closet wanting to wear a skirt that I could fit again after losing some weight but all the while knowing it was just a hair too short. I tried and tried to talk myself into it being alright, knowing that when I sat down I'd have to put my Bible over my knees. It was just so cute. I had a hard talk with myself that Sunday morning, yes I talk to myself sometimes, and I ended up giving it away and thereby winning a small victory over temptation.

If you're occasionally wearing things like my skirt that you know are even just a little indecent hoping that no one notices, trust me they do. Save yourself the worry and constant adjustment. No one enjoys spending all day yanking on their clothes, either pulling a skirt or dress down or a top up. Plus, everyone notices that you can't talk, walk or sit without adjusting yourself. It's nerve wracking for everyone involved.

If you are getting dressed for others to notice it might not be the attention you desire. When we were dating, my now husband, took me to a really nice restaurant and I wore a dress that I knew was too low cut, but I pinned it with safety pins and put a little bolero jacket over it. As we were leaving the parking garage and heading to the restaurant, I was walking with my hand over my chest and pulling on my jacket a man walked past me and said, 'If you are going to cover up you shouldn't have worn it.' Huh? No one was talking to him. I did not say one word to him why on earth was he giving me commentary on my outfit? I didn't want his attention but my dress and actions spoke to him for me and he responded. I've said it before and I'll mention it again God doesn't see as we see. He doesn't look on outward appearances but on the heart. So let's make sure we check our intentions next time we pass a mirror instead of our hair. What are your clothes telling people about you?

Likewise, what are your actions and the way you behave telling people about you? Your behavior reveals your character. Remember our definition of modesty, "Having or showing regard for the decencies of behavior, speech, dress, etc." Your speech and behavior are as integral to your modesty as your choice in clothing. Our definition says that a modest person has respect or shows regard for decent speech and behavior. Below are some indecent forms of speech or behavior that we can work on avoiding.

• **Gossiping**- 1 Tim 5:13 says, "And besides they learn to be idle, wandering about from house to house, and not only idle but also gossips and busybodies, saying things which they ought not." This verse is talking about young widows but it says of gossiping that it's saying things that you know you shouldn't. One of my favorite acronyms is T.H.I.N.K; I don't know who created it but it stays in my mind whenever I am faced with a dilemma on whether or not I should say something. Write it down and remember it next time you come to a conversational dilemma.

T- Is it true?
H- Is it helpful?
I- Is it inspiring?
N- Is it necessary?
K- Is it kind?

Next time you want to tell something you heard T.H.I.N.K first.

• **Filthy Language**- Col. 3:8 says, "But now you yourselves are to put off all these: anger, wrath, malice, blasphemy, filthy language out of your mouth. Filthy language can ruin even the most modestly dressed girls' appearance. I'm sure at some point you've seen the vapid vixens on reality television that do nothing but curse, yell and take the Lord's name in vain; who do you know that would call any of them modest? Women seem to have lost the art of being feminine. They no longer know the meaning of demure let alone have a desire to be it. But that is not so of women who style their soul. Modest women know how to use their inside voices and not bring unnecessary attention to themselves. Not only does the Bible command us to remove it from our mouths; it's also unattractive for anyone to hear a lady telling dirty jokes or cursing like a sailor.

• **Blasphemy**- We'll note Col. 3:8 again because it said to put blasphemy out of your mouth. But blasphemy is not only being irreverent towards God, it's being irreverent or reviling holy things as well. In Numbers 12:2 Miriam and Aaron speak against Moses saying, "So they said, 'Has the LORD indeed spoken only through Moses? Has He not spoken through us also?" Then verse 3 says that the Lord heard it. In verses 8-10 God says, "I speak with him face to face, even plainly, and not in dark sayings; and he sees the form of the LORD. Why then were you not afraid to speak against My servant Moses?" So the anger of the LORD was aroused against them, and He departed. And when the cloud departed from above the tabernacle, suddenly Miriam became leprous, as white as snow. Then Aaron turned toward Miriam, and there she was, a leper." Oh be careful little mouths what you say. A modest woman knows that to respect the establishments and laws of God is to respect God. Just because the world has shortened taking the Lord's name in vain to a three letter acronym does not make the use of it acceptable for worship worthy girls. We want to always be in a position of giving honor and respect to God, not disrespecting Him or His name.

• **Lying**- Rev. 21:8 says, "But the cowardly, unbelieving, abominable, murderers, sexually immoral, sorcerers, idolaters, and all liars shall have their part in the lake which burns with fire and brimstone, which is the second death." God puts liars in the same category with murderers and idolaters because Prov. 6:17 says, that God hates a lying tongue. There are no such things as white lies.

If someone asks you a leading question that you're uncomfortable answering like, 'Do I look good in this?' Don't answer immediately; just remain silent. Then answer them with a question like, 'What do you think?' Or you could tell them the truth in love with a reply like, 'No, that doesn't flatter your figure and I am telling you because I'd hope you'd tell me if I didn't look good in something.' Whatever the question is be honest with your friends because you may be the only person they ask. Lying is never an option; honesty is not the best policy it's the only policy.

Renew Your Mind

Because your thoughts determine your actions and your actions reveal your character you need to renew your mind. What have you hidden in your heart? Your heart is your spiritual mind and it needs to be renewed daily to keep it clear of the filth of the world. One way to renew your mind is to meditate on God's word. Psalm 1:1-2 is a wonderful example of a person who meditates on God's word. Psalm 1:1-2 says, "Blessed is the man who walks not in the counsel of the ungodly, nor stands in the path of sinners, nor sits in the seat of the scornful; but his delight is in the law of the LORD. And in His law he meditates day and night."

When was the last time you meditated on the scriptures? I mean took a big bite and chewed on it all day or even all week long? Mediating is not simply reading; it's finding out what the scripture you're reading means, looking up words you don't understand and figuring out if or how it applies to you. Meditating on the scriptures will help us avoid participating in the works of the flesh, Gal. 5:19-21. It will be much harder to be jealous, have an angry outburst or practice selfish ambitions if you are constantly chewing on the word of God. You can't gossip or use filthy language with a mouth full of God's word. James 4:8 says, "Draw near to God and He will draw near to you. Cleanse your hands, you sinners; and purify your hearts, you double-minded."

Likewise the long lasting flavor of the word of God will make it easier to produce fruit of the spirit, Gal. 5:22-26. It's interesting that they are referred to as works of the flesh and fruit of the spirit. You are not growing anything when you partake in works of the flesh.

Another good practice in renewing your mind is praying. Phil. 4:6-7 says, "Be anxious for nothing, but in everything by prayer and supplication, with thanksgiving, let your requests be made known to God; and the peace of God, which surpasses all understanding, will guard your hearts and minds through Christ Jesus." Prayer grants you God's peace and God's peace guards your heart and mind.

Reconsider what it is you pray for most often. How much better off would we all be if more of us prayed for wisdom instead of wealth. James 1:5 says, "If any of you lacks wisdom, let him ask of God, who gives to all liberally and without reproach, and it will be given to him." Ask not what God can do for you but what you can do for God.

Renewing your mind means getting rid of worldly thoughts and influences, but you also have to replace them with spiritual thoughts. Just like becoming healthy means cutting out junk food, sodas and fried foods; you must replace them with fruits and vegetables. Phil. 4:8 says, "Finally, brethren, whatever things are true, whatever things are noble, whatever things are just, whatever things are pure, whatever things are lovely, whatever things are of good report, if there is any virtue and if there is anything praiseworthy—think on these things." Thinking on these things listed will not only help you to renew your own mind it will benefit those you interact with daily.

The big problem that the women in 1. Tim. 2:9 were having is the same problem many women who we would deem immodest today are having and that is they need to change the channel from Me TV to Christ Central. When we spend all of our time on Me TV we can't focus on anyone or anything else. People who watch Me TV generally use words like "I, me and my" a lot. Have you ever considered what others may think or feel about your behavior or choice of clothing? Matthew 5:28 stresses the importance of changing the channel. It says that if a man looks at a woman to lust after her he has committed adultery in his heart. And this verse is not just for Christian men or only when we are in worship. This scripture is for all men even when we're are at the job or the gym. What responsibility does that put on us as women?

We're supposed to be professing godliness with good works. You may not know it but not dressing and behaving provocatively, or in a way to draw attention to yourself, could be considered a good work. If you come to worship wearing what my husband calls a Mr. T starter set around your neck, don't you think it might draw some attention away from Christ? Or if you go to school with a skirt so mini that you can't bend down when you drop your pencil, don't you think that will draw attention away from the lesson? Or if you go to work and are constantly flirting with all of the male employees, don't you think that will draw attention away from the company's mission? Some ladies simply are not thinking about others when they leave their homes for school, work or worship; they haven't changed the channel. Think of your Heavenly Father, your spiritual family, your physical family and yourself before you get dressed, speak or act because if it is done immodestly you will be professing someone, but it won't be Christ.

In the movie "The Little Mermaid" the main character, Ariel, asks the villain, Ursula, how she will get the prince to notice her without her voice and Ursula answers 'Don't underestimate the importance of body language.' Sometimes it's the villains that lay down the wisdom. We must never underestimate our body language. It's a scientific fact that women are attracted to what they hear and men to what they see. It's the reason guys practice pick up lines and we take hours to get dressed. We've already discussed the importance of our speech in regard to our modest outlook, but body language is actually a form of speech. The way you sit, stand, walk and lean all convey a message to the person you're "talking to" and others that observe you. If you sit with your legs spread I can guarantee that the opposite sex has noticed and is now thinking about your open legs. These are not the types of thoughts you want your brothers to have as you are supposed to be helping to keep their hearts pure.

Women are blessed by God with natural curves and figures not given to men but if you're walking exaggerates your natural curves to the point of distraction how is that helping your brothers? Body language speaks for your character the same way your clothes do. What does your body language tell other people when they see you? It could say you're bored by having your head thrown back and your arms crossed, it could say you're sleepy if your head keeps falling forward or it could say you're available if you "smile with your eyes as they say in modeling, and you put an extra sway in your hips and you flip your hair a lot. Our body language can quickly take us from professing godliness with good works to professing a willingness to do impure things. Even if you aren't willing, your body language will relay that message and men will respond and treat you according to that message.

1 Cor. 9:27 says, "But I discipline my body and bring it into subjection, lest, when I have preached to others, I myself should become disqualified." Self control is one of the fruit of the spirit we mentioned earlier in Gal. 5. It's difficult but it must be done; practice makes perfect. Prov. 22:1 says, "A good name is to be chosen rather than great riches, Loving favor rather than silver and gold."

Your character and reputation is your most precious commodity; you do not want anyone else to run it through the mud and you certainly don't want to ruin your own reputation because you couldn't control your body. Even though the Bible says in Matt. 7:1-2, "Judge not, that you be not judged. For with what judgment you judge, you will be judged; and with the measure you use, it will be measured back to you," people are quick to do it. While the Bible does teach righteous judging, sometimes you only get one chance with some people. Listen to Ursula, just not the way she meant it, and don't underestimate the influence of your body language on the opposite sex.

Modesty like anything else comes with practice. While we cannot throw out everything in our closets and go and buy completely new wardrobes today we can make a decision today to get rid of the tight, short, low, showy, pompous and otherwise ill fitting items in our closets. We can make a decision to actively work on not gossiping, lying or using filthy language. We can work on not attempting to attract the attention of the opposite sex by acting seductively.

A modest mind will not only affect the way you dress; it will affect your speech, thoughts, actions and outlook on life. Everything about you starts from within. You have to constantly be aware that you represent God. You are the light of the world and the last thing you want is for your clothing or actions to dim your light.

Questions

1. What's the definition of modesty?

2. How can you guard your mind?

3. How does Jesus say a person is defiled? Matt. 15:17-18

4. What does it mean to renew your mind?

5. Is there ever a time or occasion when immodesty is alright?

Chapter 6

What About Your Friends?

Christian women are all about authenticity. We worship in truth and we want to walk with true friends. I love this quote by R. Carr, "Show me your friends and I'll show you your future," because it's so very true. How many of your friends have you seen go down a dark path and get drawn away into things they shouldn't? It happens so often and so easily because of powerful, worldly influences. We have to make absolutely sure that the friends we have are going in the same direction as us and that we can be positive influences in their lives.

Signs Of A True Friend

As a preacher's child I moved around a lot and found myself constantly having to make new friends. On one such occasion in eighth grade I started school at Clemons Middle. Being the new girl is not really any fun because everyone is sizing you up and staring, you don't know anyone and have no one to talk to but the teachers; they have to be nice to you. So imagine my surprise when a girl came up to me, introduced herself and welcomed me to the school. Yay, no more only talking to teachers! We were in the library after she introduced herself, talking, when three girls approached us. I thought yay more friends but I was sadly mistaken.

The leader of this group promptly declared that if she were me she wouldn't talk to my new friend. She gave me the chance to hang with her instead. No introductions, she wanted me to look out for my budding popularity. Apparently my new friend was not winning any votes for most popular. A line had been drawn right in the middle of the library, what should I do? Everyone wants to be accepted and sit at the popular table, right?

Do I ditch the girl, who thirty seconds ago was a friendly angel or do I risk being shunned by the self-proclaimed cool girls because of a social hierarchy I was too new to know about? Decisions, decisions. Luckily for me I've never been one to take things at face value. Plus, I have extensive knowledge of what it feels like to be left out so I've never been one for leaving others out. So, I very matter of factly told the friend thieving threesome that I was perfectly capable of choosing my own friends. I then took my new friend by the hand and walked off with my Christianity intact.

Now, for arguments sake, let's imagine if I had ditched my new friend for the self proclaimed cool girls. How long do you think it would've been before I was acting like them in order to remain in their good graces? How would my ex friend have felt after she'd taken the chance to welcome me and I'd left her at the first sign of something that seemed better? You want to make sure your friends are the type of people you wouldn't mind emulating. True friends back you up and raise you up.

Daniel is a person in the Bible who was a true friend and had the right kind of friends. Let's read the first chapter of Daniel together and check out what made him a good friend and exactly what kinds of friends he had.

"In the third year of the reign of Jehoiakim king of Judah, Nebuchadnezzar king of Babylon came to Jerusalem and besieged it. And the Lord gave Jehoiakim king of Judah into his hand, with some of the articles of the house of God, which he carried into the land of Shinar to the house of his god; and he brought the articles into the treasure house of his god. Then the king instructed Ashpenaz, the master of his eunuchs, to bring some of the children of Israel and some of the king's descendants and some of the nobles, young men in whom there was no blemish, but good-looking, gifted in all wisdom, possessing knowledge and quick to understand, who had ability to serve in the king's palace, and whom they might teach the language and literature of the Chaldeans. And the king appointed for them a daily provision of the king's delicacies and of the wine which he drank, and three years of training for them, so that at the end of that time they might serve before the king.

Now from among those of the sons of Judah were Daniel, Hananiah, Mishael, and Azariah. To them the chief of the eunuchs gave names: he gave Daniel the name Belteshazzar; to Hananiah, Shadrach; to Mishael, Meshach; and to Azariah, Abed-Nego. But Daniel purposed in his heart that he would not defile himself with the portion of the king's delicacies, nor with the wine which he drank; therefore he requested of the chief of the eunuchs that he might not defile himself. Now God had brought Daniel into the favor and goodwill of the chief of the eunuchs. And the chief of the eunuchs said to Daniel, "I fear my lord the king, who has appointed your food and drink. For why should he see your faces looking worse than the young men who are your age? Then you would endanger my head before the king."

So Daniel said to the steward whom the chief of the eunuchs had set over Daniel, Hananiah, Mishael, and Azariah, "Please test your servants for ten days, and let them give us vegetables to eat and water to drink. Then let our appearance be examined before you, and the appearance of the young men who eat the portion of the king's delicacies; and as you see fit, so deal with your servants." So he consented with them in this matter, and tested them ten days. And at the end of ten days their features appeared better and fatter in flesh than all the young men who ate the portion of the king's delicacies.

Thus the steward took away their portion of delicacies and the wine that they were to drink, and gave them vegetables. As for these four young men, God gave them knowledge and skill in all literature and wisdom; and

Daniel had understanding in all visions and dreams. Now at the end of the days, when the king had said that they should be brought in, the chief of the eunuchs brought them in before Nebuchadnezzar. Then the king interviewed them, and among them all none was found like Daniel, Hananiah, Mishael, and Azariah; therefore they served before the king. And in all matters of wisdom and understanding about which the king examined them, he found them ten times better than all the magicians and astrologers who were in all his realm. Thus Daniel continued until the first year of King Cyrus."

As you read in verse 8 Daniel purposed in his heart not to defile himself. He made up his mind and decided before the situation arose that he would remain pure and free from sin. Jews under the old law couldn't eat certain meats so when Daniel was presented with them they were a non issue for him. Daniel could've remained quiet had he not already decided to remain pure or he could've just asked for himself to be excused from the king's delicacies and told his friends they were on their own. But we see in verse 12 that Daniel wasn't that kind of guy. He asked for all of his friends to be able to remain pure like he'd planned for himself. He was a good friend and helped them rise to the occasion through his good example.

Shadrach, Meshach and Abed-Nego were good friends to Daniel because they had his back. When he made his proposal they didn't take three steps back and tell him he was on his own. They trusted his judgment, quietly accepted the challenge and didn't sin against God. Then in verses 15-16 we see that the experiment worked in their favor and God blessed them all. Go back and read verses 8 and 12 again. The first chapter of Daniel is a perfect example of the kind of friend we want to be and the kind of friends we want to have around us.

Friends Don't Let Friends Sin

In Daniel 3 we get another insight into their friendship. Shadrach, Meshach and Abed-Nego have been put into positions of power through

God's blessings, (Dan. 2:49) and they ruled over provinces because Daniel petitioned the king on their behalf; they also stayed true to God. They weren't too old to band together, trust each other and stand by one another. Their earlier test only served to cement their friendship and faith. They were more than ready for the next obstacle.

Let's read Dan. 3 to find out how they overcame, "Nebuchadnezzar the king made an image of gold, whose height was sixty cubits and its width six cubits. He set it up in the plain of Dura, in the province of Babylon. And King Nebuchadnezzar sent word to gather together the satraps, the administrators, the governors, the counselors, the treasurers, the judges, the magistrates, and all the officials of the provinces, to come to the dedication of the image which King Nebuchadnezzar had set up. So the satraps, the administrators, the governors, the counselors, the treasurers, the judges, the magistrates, and all the officials of the provinces gathered together for the dedication of the image that King Nebuchadnezzar had set up; and they stood before the image that Nebuchadnezzar had set up.

Then a herald cried aloud: "To you it is commanded, O peoples, nations, and languages, that at the time you hear the sound of the horn, flute, harp, lyre, and psaltery, in symphony with all kinds of music, you shall fall down and worship the gold image that King Nebuchadnezzar has set up; and whoever does not fall down and worship shall be cast immediately into the midst of a burning fiery furnace." So at that time, when all the people heard the sound of the horn, flute, harp, and lyre, in symphony with all kinds of music, all the people, nations, and languages fell down and worshiped the gold image which King Nebuchadnezzar had set up.

Therefore at that time certain Chaldeans came forward and accused the Jews. They spoke and said to King Nebuchadnezzar, "O king, live forever! You, O king, have made a decree that everyone who hears the sound of the horn, flute, harp, lyre, and psaltery, in symphony with all kinds of music, shall fall down and worship the gold image; and whoever does not fall down and worship shall be cast into the midst of a burning fiery furnace. There are certain Jews whom you have set over the affairs of the province of Babylon: Shadrach, Meshach, and Abed-Nego; these men, O king, have not paid due regard to you.

They do not serve your gods or worship the gold image which you have set up." Then Nebuchadnezzar, in rage and fury, gave the command to bring Shadrach, Meshach, and Abed-Nego. So they brought these men before the king. Nebuchadnezzar spoke, saying to them, "Is it true, Shadrach, Meshach, and Abed-Nego, that you do not serve my gods or worship the gold image which I have set up? Now if you are ready at the time you hear the sound of the horn, flute, harp, lyre, and psaltery, in symphony with all kinds of music, and you fall down and worship the image which I have made, good! But if you do not worship, you shall be cast immediately into the midst of a burning fiery furnace. And who is the god who will deliver you from my hands?" Shadrach, Meshach, and Abed-Nego answered and said to the king, "O Nebuchadnezzar, we have no need to answer you in this matter. If that is the case, our God whom we serve is able to deliver us from the burning fiery furnace, and He will deliver us from your hand, O king. But if not, let it be known to you, O king, that we do not serve your gods, nor will we worship the gold image which you have set up."

Then Nebuchadnezzar was full of fury, and the expression on his face changed toward Shadrach, Meshach, and Abed-Nego. He spoke and commanded that they heat the furnace seven times more than it was usually heated. And he commanded certain mighty men of valor who were in his army to bind Shadrach, Meshach, and Abed-Nego, and cast them into the burning fiery furnace. Then these men were bound in their coats, their trousers, their turbans, and their other garments, and were cast into the midst of the burning fiery furnace.

Therefore, because the king's command was urgent, and the furnace exceedingly hot, the flame of the fire killed those men who took up Shadrach, Meshach, and Abed-Nego. And these three men, Shadrach, Meshach, and Abed-Nego, fell down bound into the midst of the burning fiery furnace.

Then King Nebuchadnezzar was astonished; and he rose in haste and spoke, saying to his counselors, "Did we not cast three men bound into the midst of the fire?" They answered and said to the king, "True, O king." "Look!" he answered, "I see four men loose, walking in the midst of the fire; and they are not hurt, and the form of the fourth is like the Son of God."

Then Nebuchadnezzar went near the mouth of the burning fiery furnace and spoke, saying, "Shadrach, Meshach, and Abed-Nego, servants of the Most High God, come out, and come here." Then Shadrach, Meshach, and Abed-Nego came from the midst of the fire. And the satraps, administrators, governors, and the king's counselors gathered together, and they saw these men on whose bodies the fire had no power; the hair of their head was not singed nor were their garments affected, and the smell of fire was not on them. Nebuchadnezzar spoke, saying, "Blessed be the God of Shadrach, Meshach, and Abed-Nego, who sent His Angel and delivered His servants who trusted in Him, and they have frustrated the king's word, and yielded their bodies, that they should not serve nor worship any god except their own God! Therefore I make a decree that any people, nation, or language which speaks anything amiss against the God of Shadrach, Meshach, and Abed-Nego shall be cut in pieces, and their houses shall be made an ash heap; because there is no other God who can deliver like this." Then the king promoted Shadrach, Meshach, and Abed-Nego in the province of Babylon."

The only reason three young men would willingly walk into an oven so hot that the men charged with opening the doors were burned up is their shared belief and trust in the Almighty. If it came to a point in our country where Christians could be openly persecuted, would your current friends stand by you like Shadrach, Meshach and Abed-Nego? Would you stand by Christ? Think of how frightened these guys must've been. I'm sure they knew it was only a matter of time before someone noticed they weren't bowing down. Do you think any of them thought about just giving in and bowing down?

Eccl. 4:9-10, 12 says, "Two are better than one, because they have a good reward for their labor. For if they fall, one will lift up his companion. But woe to him who is alone when he falls, for he has no one to help him up. Though one may be overpowered by another, two can withstand him. And a threefold cord is not quickly broken." The Bible says there is strength in numbers and each of them kept the other confident and faithful.

You need friends that will help you when you're weak not ones that will say I thought you were a Christian, when you stumble. Those young men faced death head on. They'd just seen what happened to the ones opening the oven and still persevered together. And you know what happened, you just read it, God brought them through their trial together.

Life is the same for girls and women who are walking worthy to worship their King. You'll encounter so many situations that will try and tempt you to waver and stray from God. You must decide for yourself how much your relationship with God means to you. Will you be like Daniel and decide in your heart that no matter the situation you're in or the people you're around, you'll not defile yourself? Can you make a commitment to protect yourself from the deceptions of the world by trusting that God knows what's best for you in all areas of life?

I'm sure the king's delicacies and meats were beautifully arrayed, buffet style and on gorgeous table cloths and gold platters. Unfortunately that is how sin is displayed. It looks good from afar, it's displayed beautifully and everyone partaking looks like they're having so much fun. Until you get close and see that behind that love story is fornication; inside that under dog triumph is deception. Once you get close you'll see that all that glitters isn't gold and if you partake of it all that happens is you become defiled.

1. Cor. 15:33-34 says, "Do not be deceived: "Evil company corrupts good habits." Awake to righteousness, and do not sin; for some do not have the knowledge of God. I speak this to your shame." And 1. Cor. 5:11 says, "But now I have written to you not to keep company with anyone named a brother, who is sexually immoral, or covetous, or an idolater, or a reviler, or a drunkard, or an extortioner—not even to eat with such a person."

It is vital that you surround yourself with people who will build you up, encourage you in your walk and stand by you when difficult situations come. You want friends who will tell you the truth in love, sometimes even give a little tough love. Daniel pulled his friends along with him and you should try to keep your friends from giving into their lusts, just like you want them to steer you away from yours. James 1:13-15 says, "Let no one say when he is tempted, "I am tempted by God"; for God cannot be tempted by evil, nor does He Himself tempt anyone. But each one is tempted when he is drawn away by his own desires and enticed. Then, when desire has conceived, it gives birth to sin; and sin, when it is full-grown, brings forth death." And James 5:16 says, "Confess your trespasses to one another, and pray for one another, that you may be healed. The effective, fervent prayer of a righteous man avails much."

Of course now we all have friends who have not yet come to Christ for forgiveness of sins. I'm not telling you to shun them. Perhaps by your good example they'll be won to Christ. You just want to make sure that your closest friends, the ones with the highest potential for influence, are people like Shadrach, Meshach and Abed-Nego. As we quoted at the beginning of this chapter, "Show me your friends and I'll show you your future." Does your future look bright?

Questions

1. What does Daniel teach you about being a friend?

2. What do you learn about the type of friends you should have from Shadrach, Meshach and Abed-Nego?

3. Paying close attention to your current friends how does your future look?

4. What difficult situation have you overcome with the help of your friends?

Part 3
Wardrobe

Chapter 7

Purposefully Adorned

What's your purpose when you get dressed? You could say that it depends on where you're going and what you're going to do. And while you wouldn't wear a fur coat to the beach or red to a funeral, the place or activity does not determine your purpose. We've discussed modesty in a previous chapter and how it begins in your mind, your purpose is no different. Eccl. 3:1 says, "To everything there is a season and a time for every purpose under heaven." Remember this, write it on your mirror if need be, your purpose when getting dressed is to respect God, yourself and others. 1. Tim 2:10 says to dress in such a way as to profess Godliness. That is your purpose when getting dressed no matter where you are going or what you're going to do.

Everyone's style is different. I myself am girly and laid back. As my husband says I like anything with a ruffle. But I also like to dress comfortably and those style parameters are the basis for my wardrobe. But being purposefully adorned doesn't have anything to do with your personal style it has more to do with your style intentions.

Some get dressed solely for the purpose of getting men to look their way. So they have no reservations about baring their belly, wearing dresses that should be shirts or skirts that are in fact meant to be belts. But getting dressed for men to look at you doesn't respect God (1. Pet. 3:3-5), it doesn't respect you (Prov. 11:22) and it doesn't respect the guys you're trying to attract (Prov. 7:10-27).

Queen Vashti, in the book of Esther, was asked to come to the king's feast full of drunken men and show her beauty. Let's read what happened in Esther 1:10-12, "On the seventh day, when the heart of the king was merry with wine, he commanded Mehuman, Biztha, Harbona, Bigtha, Abagtha, Zethar, and Carcas, seven eunuchs who served in the presence of King Ahasuerus, to bring Queen Vashti before the king, wearing her royal crown, in order to show her beauty to the people and the officials, for she was beautiful to behold. But Queen Vashti refused to come at the king's command brought by his eunuchs; therefore the king was furious, and his anger burned within him." The Bible doesn't say exactly how the king wanted Vashti dressed to show her beauty, but she deserves immense respect for standing up for herself and not parading around for a group of drunken men.

Well, what about getting dressed to look good? The fact that girls and women want to look their best is not a secret; we were made that way. Desiring to look your best is never an issue. Everyone is beautiful in their own way. The problems arise when looking your best becomes everything to you. How many celebrities are only famous because of how they look? You know it, I know it and they know it. They bring no special talents to the table and they haven't invented anything; they just look good. Prov. 31:30 says, "Charm is deceitful and beauty is passing but a woman that fears the Lord she shall be praised." Unfortunately for many celebrities their life, work, money and worth is tied to their passing looks. It's fading and while they'll use any cream necessary the Bible says it won't last.

I believe that everyone should try and look their best and feel good about themselves. Vincent Van Gough said, "There is no such thing as an ugly woman." Just be mindful so that looking good doesn't become your sole purpose when getting dressed.

Remembering your true purpose of respecting God, yourself and others when getting dressed will help you in all clothing related aspects of your life. When you go shopping, remembering your purpose will help in deciding what to buy and what to leave. It'll help you as you face your closet in the morning and wonder what to wear and it'll help you on Sunday morning as you look in the mirror and wonder is this outfit worthy to be in the presence of the Almighty God?

Going to worship has become a perilous adventure for young men. They are constantly told to keep their minds pure, so they come to the place that's supposed to help them with that task. But their very sisters become their enemies. How can a young man keep his mind clean when he can, not only see ample cleavage, but legs for days. There are bra straps peeking at him from every angle and sheer fabric to entice him to consider what's underneath. How can he effectively keep his eyes and thoughts on the cross when he is being tempted by teen girls and their moms?

Look around you on Sunday morning, maybe while in the lobby, and pretend you're a guy and notice how many girls and women are wearing distracting clothing. You'll gain a greater appreciation for a guy's plight. In Gen 4:9 Cain asks God is he his brother's keeper? What do you think? Are we our brother's keepers? 1. Cor. 8:13 talks about not causing a brother to stumble. Have you, like Cain, been killing your brother's conscience, wondering what his problem is and then asking God if you're his keeper?

At the beginning of this book we talked about worship, true worship and vain worship. When we worship we bring God a sacrifice, the sacrifice of ourselves and our obedience. We must be sure to bring our sacrifices in a package worthy to offer to God. We wouldn't take a present to the President and First Lady in a garbage bag. We wouldn't go on an interview and hand the potential employer a crumpled, soda stained or ripped up resume. Remember where you are and why you're there. Your purpose when getting dressed is especially important when going before God.

Rom. 12:1 says, "I beseech you therefore, brethren, by the mercies of

God, that you present your bodies a living sacrifice, holy, acceptable to God, which is your reasonable service." It's reasonable or rational for us to serve and dedicate our lives to God based on what He has done for us. He's not asking too much. Micah 6:8 says, "He has shown you, o man, what is good; and what does the Lord require of you but to do justly, to love mercy, and to walk humbly with your God?"

On Sundays we bring our living sacrifice to God, but we don't live in the building. Being purposefully adorned is for the rest of the week as well. Paul says you're a living sacrifice and you should not conform to the world and their ideas or standards. Basically not every trend is for you, and you need to live everyday worthy of your calling (Eph. 4:1). Being purposefully adorned everyday means going to the gym wearing appropriate clothes for the activity and for your purpose. You go to school wearing clothes that reflect your style and purpose. No matter where you go as long as your purpose is in the front of your mind you won't go wrong.

Closet Confidential

A closet can be many things, a welcoming retreat a relaxing oasis or a chaotic catastrophe. Mine is currently the latter. There are clothes everywhere and that fact could be a red flag to two scenarios. I either have too many clothes or I'm a slob; I'm going to choose the first. I've heard it said that we can only use 80% of our closets and out of that 80% we only wear 20% regularly. Armed with that knowledge I want to introduce you to the closet catharsis. A catharsis is "The purging of the emotions or relieving of emotional tensions, especially through certain kinds of art (Dictionary.com)." Basically we, yes you and I, are going to rid our lives of things that we can no longer fit, clothes we haven't worn in the last year and anything we've moved on from and relieve the tension and emotional baggage of clutter and confusion.

Cleaning and organizing your closet is the gateway to organizing your life and having more time for more important tasks. Imagine how much time you could save by simply knowing where key pieces are located? Also, cleansing your closet allows you to see what basic items you're missing. Finally, once your closet is cleansed you can actually use what you have rather than stand around asking the question dreaded by women all around the world, "What am I going to wear today?"

What To Toss

Pretend your closet is a fabulous boutique designed just for you. Now go inside and look around. Some items can be tossed just by looking at them, especially anything outdated or things you simply no longer like. For everything else try it on. Have fun with it. Invite a friend over to take photos of you in various outfits, because we all know pictures don't lie. Then go and do the same for her in her closet. Once you start trying things on see how they feel. Is the item too big or small, tight or short? Walk around in it, sit in it and evaluate it. Would you consider yourself purposefully adorned in it? Remember our clothes should show our respect for God, ourselves and others.

You have to be brutally honest here; make sure the friend you choose to help you evaluate has your best interests at heart. Tell your family what you're up to and put on a fashion show for the outfits you and your friend can't decide on. Don't get sad about tossing certain items. They are just taking up space, if we're not using them, and could be a blessing for someone else. Plus, you can always get new clothes; what you can't get back is a bad impression left by wearing inappropriate clothing.

Proverbs 22:1 says a good name is to be valued more than gold or silver. Once you've removed all of the clothes that are too big, too small, too tight, too short or too out of style go back through your closet one more time. I know, I know, but make sure you're not holding onto anything unnecessarily.

Now, that your closet has been cleansed, it's time to put away what's left. You can choose any system you like, but choose one. Your closet can be arranged by color, article of clothing or by season. I bet you're still left with a pretty decent wardrobe. Bag up the items you've decided to toss and take them to your congregation's clothing donation room, donate them to the Goodwill or find out if a missionary is in need of clothing. Don't forget to hang up accessories and make a place for everything in your closet.

What To Add

We've noted that everyone's personal style is different but there are some pieces that everyone needs in their wardrobe no matter personal style. These are a few key and basic pieces that will help you maintain your purpose. These are pieces anyone who truly wants to style their soul is going to need in their closet to save them from embarrassment.

• **Tank Tops**- You want quality so think J. Crew, New York & Co. and Ann Taylor, but shop stores like T.J. Maxx, Ross and Marshalls for them at a discount. These tanks are made of high quality material that stretch and retain their shape after many wears and washes. Also, the necklines tend to be higher and they are generally not sheer.

• **Bolero**- Many dresses today are sleeveless and sometimes it's not a problem because the straps are wide enough but other times you need a cover up. These half jackets usually have short or ¾ length sleeves and come in cotton and denim for more casual wear or satin for more formal events. They look great on almost all body shapes and are a wonderful alternative to a full jacket.

• **Cardigan-** Another amazing option for covering shoulders and arms. I love cardigans because they come in so many fun prints and work extremely well to fight off the chill without being bulky.

• **Plain White T-shirt**- They're not just for guys and they fit under and over almost anything. I personally don't wear spaghetti strapped items, but plain white tees are great for going under shirts or dresses with thin straps.

• **Slips**- Everyone needs a full slip and a half slip. The popular designers today are not designing for soul stylists like us and sometimes you put on a dress and when the sun hits it you can see straight through it. Even dresses that have 'built-in- slips' still occasionally need extra help. Slips also help to hide panty lines, which are unseemly.

• **Black And White Undies**- While not as popular as the ruffled or neon green pair, everyone needs solid colored bras and panties. The last thing you want is to have your hot pink bra showing through your shirt.

These are just everyday pieces to add to ensure that whatever you wear can be decent and modest. How many times have you seen some part of a girl and wished you hadn't? Maybe she didn't put on a slip and you could see straight through her dress or maybe she decided to wear hot pink underwear with white pants. Whatever it was, being out and indecent is uncomfortable and embarrassing for the one who wore it and the people who saw it. And be honest many times when you leave the house unprepared you are just stuck. You can't go back home to change and you certainly don't have a change of clothes with you. This is why it is so important to triple check yourself before you leave the house.

• **Check One**- Put your hands inside the garment, in a well lit room, to see if you can see your fingers through it and adjust accordingly.

• **Check Two-** After taking the necessary precautions look at yourself again in a well-lit room. Don't get dressed in the dark no matter how early it is, and look at yourself in a full-length mirror, front and back.

• **Check Three-** Ask a family member's opinion before you dash out of the house. Just have someone give you a once over to ensure you're safe from embarrassment and embarrassing others.

Save yourself and make time for this three point style inspection. Always put something on that reflects your purpose for getting dressed. Get rid of items that are holding you and your closet back from truly representing God. Add items that truly show your respect for God, yourself and others. By doing all of these things you can actually present yourself to God as a living sacrifice.

Questions

1. What is your purpose when getting dressed?

2. How can you become your brother's keeper?

3. What does God require of you? Micah 6:8

4. Have you committed to your closet catharsis? When will you start?

5. Write and remember the three point inspection to avoid wardrobe malfunctions.

Chapter 8

The Ten Commandments of Shopping

As a Christian, shopping can be tough work. The world's standard of modesty, decency and dress are hardly aligned with our standard. It's difficult sometimes to find pretty and trendy pieces that also fit our purpose for getting dressed. That's why I've created these ten shopping commandments to help you navigate the retail waters and make purchases you won't regret.

#1 You Shall Buy In Bulk

When I was a teen I had a cap sleeved, scoop neck, ankle length, blue flowered dress. You see how well I am still able to describe it even though I haven't had that dress in over ten years; basically I loved that dress. I felt beautiful in it. But one Sunday morning my friend's younger sister asked me if I owned any other dresses. She said, "You wear that dress almost every Sunday. Do you not have any others to wear?" Well embarrassing doesn't really seem to do my feelings justice. Of course I had other dresses but why couldn't she see how fantastic this one was? Needless to say in my youthful ignorance I'd made the chief rookie shopper mistake; I only bought one.

When you find something that you love, a dress in my case, the number one commandment is to buy in bulk. Don't think Costco, I mean we just cleansed our closets. But if you happen to find an essential piece like an A-line skirt, a great pair of pants or a terrific tank buy more than one and if possible in a few colors. Perfect pieces are few and far so when you stumble upon a perfect for you item, get more than one.

#2 You Shall Always Try Things On

I don't know the words to accurately describe the level of hatred I have for trying on clothes; I loathe it. That being said just because you don't like something doesn't mean you shouldn't do it if it's helpful. For instance trying on clothes will save you from my most current dilemma. I have in my possession a pair of jeans that need to be returned to one store and a dress that needs to be returned to another. One item now has a stain on it and the other's receipt is missing. Pay attention to the nonsense and wasted time that occurs when you don't try on items in the store, and avoid my mistakes.

Trying on things also helps you to know what shapes, patterns and colors look best on you. Pick a store whose aesthetic you admire and just go in and try on a few items. Either choose them based on the way their styled on mannequins or ask a salesperson to choose some pieces that will look best on you based on your body shape. You don't have to buy anything on this trip just get an idea of what types of cuts and styles you like and which ones look great on you. Take some photos with your phone's camera for reference. Even if you can't afford the outfits you now have a handy look book of styles you know you look good in.

#3 You Shall Shop Where You Think You Can't Afford To Shop

I know how it sounds, calm down. I'm not telling you to go into debt over clothes, but shopping at the stores that you think you can't afford is truly the best advice you can receive. On one such shopping excursion my friend and I were shopping in Lenox Mall in Atlanta; in case you've never been there they have a Louis Vuitton, Fendi, Bulgari and Cartier store inside. It's full of high end specialty stores in addition to stores like Macy's. So when my friend went into one such specialty clothing boutique I just kind of hung out near the entrance because I knew there was nothing in that store I could afford. I mean I've been to Lenox several times and had never even graced this store's entrance.

Well, my friend walked straight to the back of the store, looked around and found a gorgeous, mustard colored trench coat for about $20! I was floored and now frantically searching for one for myself. Trench coats never go out of style; they are the ultimate classic in classic pieces and since this store was a high end boutique the quality of the coat was amazing. I learned my lesson that day, everyone has a clearance rack. While the pieces that you find might not be in season, if it's a classic like a trench you'll never have to worry about whether or not you made a good purchase.

#4 You Shall Shop For Quality Not Quantity

Since our closets are now clean and free of useless, to us, items we want to complete our wardrobes with long lasting, high quality and easily mixable pieces. The key to successful shopping is making your money create value. You want to be aware of what you have already, make a list of what you need and then find accessories to finish the look. For instance you could spend $100 on ten pieces of low quality and craftsmanship that will maybe last you three months. Or you could spend that same $100 on five key, high quality pieces that can mix with the current items in your closet and will last you many years.

In the previous chapter we talked about pieces that needed to be added to your wardrobe, find the best of those items so that you won't have to continue purchasing them. When you buy lower quality items you end up spending more money because you have to replace them so frequently. When considering quality pieces think of the cost versus how many times you'll wear it and divide accordingly.

That calculation will give you the cost of the item in value and worth. Obviously something you'll only wear once will have less value, especially if it's pricey versus something you can wear many times.

#5 You Shall Consider Shopping Less Often

At a lectureship I met a woman who told me that she shops twice a year, spring and fall. At first my inner shopaholic was appalled. How could any woman only go shopping twice a year? Then she explained that she saves her money for two major shopping trips instead of tiny shopping adventures every weekend. As I thought more about it, it made perfect sense. The new fashions come out in September and March, so if you have a good chunk of change you could buy almost whatever you wanted for that season.

Now of course she couldn't find everything in one day so in actuality she shopped more than two times but what a radical idea. Not only will this mentality allow you to buy quality pieces but you can really have fun and create your look for the entire season knowing that you've saved up and aren't just out throwing away money every weekend.

#6 You Shall Know That You Never Have To Pay Full Price

For me personally one of the thrills of shopping is the joy of the hunt. I love to find high quality things at amazingly low prices. Bargain shopping in some areas is an Olympic sport. There are the professionals who can find leather Coach bags for $40 and those who can get jeans for free. Then there are the semi-pros who talk to the sales people to find out when things go on sale. Last but not least the rookies scope out the goods and wait patiently by visiting the stores a few times to see if the piece has gone on sale.

It doesn't matter where you rank as long as you know that the quoted price never has to be the selling price. Never be afraid to ask the sales person for a coupon while checking out at the register. Talk to them and find out when certain specials run and when new merchandise is displayed. Sign up for e-newsletters and mailing lists for coupons and discounts.

You can also shop at discount stores. They offer many of the same name brands and styles as department stores and for much less. While you won't be able to use coupons or get percentages off at these stores the savings in price will likely be equal or greater. Never feel like something is out of your grasp forever. Nothing stays in any store forever and eventually it will need to be discounted and sold; and now you'll be ready to score your beautiful piece at a great discount.

#7 You Shall Mix High With Low

I know I keep saying it but I really can't stress it enough quality is king. That being said there are some pieces that can be lower quality to add variety to your wardrobe. Those pieces are going to be trendy and seasonal items. Fashion changes all of the time so you don't want to constantly add every new trend to your wardrobe, but there will be some fun pieces you want to mix in.

When buying those pieces you want them to be nice but you don't have to spend a chunk of change on them because you may or may not wear it next season. Shop at trendier stores for brightly colored, bold and odd pieces and even swap trendy pieces with friends. The key here is to have fun with the latest fashions and not break the bank.

#8 You Shall Accessorize

Much like the last commandment accessories can come from a variety s. Accessories are there to complete your look; they finalize an outfit like icing on a cake. You can have lots of fun with all kinds of accessories. They can be as inexpensive as $0.99 earrings or as expensive as a $1,000 handbag. What you choose is up to you and your money. But no matter what you spend accessories are the finishing touch to any ensemble.

BAGS

From clutches to tote bags, satchels to wristlets, doctor bags to carryalls there is a bag for everyone. Your bag of choice is going to depend on where you're going and what you need with you. For purses I would encourage you to stick to the quality route. Find a well-made day bag that goes with everything. You'll reference this bag often so you'll want something in black or tan and large enough for at least your wallet, phone and keys. For special purpose bags like sequined clutches or beach bags you can go the cheaper, trendier route. In all honesty if you have two or three high quality all-purpose bags you are good to go for years. You can then add lower quality but trendier purses as you see fit.

SHOES

Unlike bags where you can mix in some high and low quality you want all of your shoes to be well made. Shoes have much more wear on them than bags and unlike bags they are wrapped around your foot. If you buy cheaper shoes they can shrink and squeeze your foot, the heel won't be durable enough for long wear and can snap under you.

A good test for shoes, especially heels, is to stand them up and gently push them. Just give them a slight nudge. If they remain standing they are probably good quality if they fall over put them back on the shelf and run. O.k. you don't have to run but leave them in the store. The comfort of y[illegible] feet is vital to making it through an entire day so from tennis shoes to h[illegible] flip flops buy the best quality you can. Shoes can lift an entire outfit.

one of the best places for investment accessories.

JEWELRY

Here's where accessorizing gets fun. From Claire's to Dillard's everyone sells jewelry and now many discount stores like Target sell beautiful pieces. For me jewelry is just fun. It can be large and make a statement or small pearl studs to help you look polished. No matter where you get your jewelry have fun with it and try lots of styles. This is really the area to try any trend because you'll always be able to find an inexpensive version of it. I personally love to pair solid color ensembles with bright bold necklaces and earrings. Above all else I must have earrings on every time I go out. For one of my sisters it's bags and for my youngest sister and aunt it's rings. They love them and the bigger the better. Whatever it is that you love go all out with it.

HATS/ GLOVES/ SCARVES

Not too many people wear hats everyday but they can be a fun addition to any wardrobe because they'll be unexpected. Gloves are the same; while in times past ladies would never leave the house without their gloves, I doubt any of us have a pair outside of winter gloves. Try out a short leather or lace pair just for fun and variety with an outfit. Scarves are much more popular today and come in all colors, patterns and fabrics. They can go a long way in jazzing up a boring outfit or hiding that lunch time mustard stain on your white shirt. Grab a few of these accessories to add some spice and panache to a few of your looks and to stand out from the crowd.

#9 You Shall Have A Style Signature

Do you have a favorite color or perfume? Does wearing that item make you smile? If so incorporate that color or fragrance into every outfit. Maybe

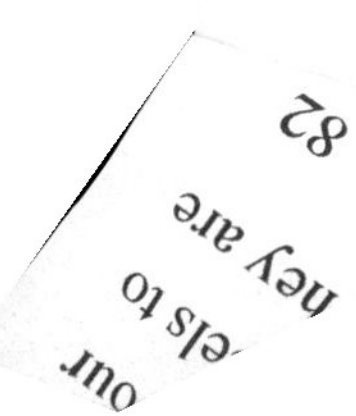

you love blue so no matter what you're wearing there will be something blue on you, even if it's a hair bow. Do you love headbands? Build up your collection and wear one every day. It doesn't have to be anything major just something that makes you smile and makes you feel good. A big part of feeling good for women is looking good.

My signature would be earrings. I just love them and need a pair to feel that I look put together. Find your signature and rock it. You don't have to tell anyone as long as it makes you happy and feel good about starting your day.

#10 You Shall Maintain Your Clothes

Like anything else clothes need maintenance and proper care. Read the labels on your clothes. Some fabrics like silk, wool and suede should only be dry cleaned. Others like cotton, nylon and blended fabrics can simply be washed at home on the gentle cycle. Pay extra attention to underwear, slips, dresses and blouses. Delicate items may even need to be hand washed depending on the fabric and durability of the piece. Put all of your underwear in one load, on the gentle cycle; it will help them avoid fraying and keep their shape. Wash like colors together, lights, whites and darks. Denim should be turned inside out and washed alone with other denim items so they don't bleed.

This command is what separates the amateurs from the pros. You want your clothes to retain their color, shape and fit. Let your clothes hang to dry if you have time because the dryer will shrink certain items. I hang my blouses, jeans, dresses and pants. T-shirts, shorts and underwear can go into the dryer. Once in the dryer use the delicate cycle to avoid shrinkage. Finally hang up everything or put it away neatly to lessen the time needed for ironing in the morning and you'll be on your way to the wardrobe of your dreams.

Bonus Commandment #11 You Shall Shine Your Light

Fashion and shopping are fun and they can serve a variety of purposes. This chapter has been all about completing your wardrobe to match your purpose for getting dressed, but fashion and shopping can also serve other purposes such as fellowship. Take out a new sister or younger sister in Christ and get to know her. Use shopping as a way to break the ice and welcome or encourage her.

Also, fashion is a great way to learn about your own style preferences. I did an experiment where I wore a dress everyday for 31 days. Of course I had some repeat looks but it was exciting and fun. I posted my looks to Facebook each day and had people follow my progress. It was an eye opening experience and has resulted in me wearing dresses a few times a week now. Go to the Facebook page, www.facebook.com/virtuousmagazine, and check out day 14; I am wearing it as I type this.

Dresses make you feel feminine, pretty and ladylike. The whole experiment came from a desire to search bygone style eras, but it's simple things that playing with fashion can teach you. Maybe you feel like Sunday is the only time you really get dressed up; if that's the case try out the 31 days of dresses experiment and dress up every day. See what transformations you experience.

My ultimate desire for you is to create a wardrobe that's welcoming and respectful of your purpose. I want you to shine your Christian light as brightly as possible and be a reflection of Christ. You don't want your outfit to dim your light. I truly believe that when you look good, you feel good and those good feelings result in you doing good for God and others.

Questions

1. List the ten commandments of shopping.

2. Why is quality king over quantity?

3. Do you have a style signature? What is it?

4. How can you use shopping to shine your light?

Chapter 9

Someone Is Watching You

I am the eldest of three sisters. Growing up they wanted to do everything that I did and go everywhere I went. If you have younger siblings then you probably understand. Since I am the oldest and I know that they will do what I do, I have to be an example to my younger sisters. The same is true for younger sisters in Christ. We have to show them God's will through our actions, speech and dress.

One sister in Christ told me one day that she'd told her daughter to watch me and to act like me. Well, she enlightened me a few years after she'd told her daughter and I was shocked. Not that I'd done anything obscene but I had no idea someone was literally walking in my footsteps and taking notes.

Being a Christian example is so important because you may be the only one some girls see. You have to let your light shine everywhere because you never know who may be watching you, from your best friend to the eight year old who hugs you every Sunday morning. You don't want someone else's light dimmed because you turned yours off for a second to do something, say something or wear something worldly.

Some congregations already have a big sister/little sister program and you can join in that work. On the other hand your little sister may be your biological sister. No matter how your mentor/mentee relationship begins you want to be extra mindful of them and your behavior. Here are five things you can do to be a role model any young Christian sister would be thrilled to have.

Remember Daniel

Daniel purposed in his heart not to sin against God before any situation ever arose. You have to do the same in regards to being a good role model. You have to decide that no matter what happens you will demonstrate a Godly example to your "little sister." Every time you talk to her you must reflect Christ and give Bible advice to her everyday life situations. Decide today that even if you don't yet have a little sister that you will walk worthy for a little sister you might not know is watching.

Think About What You Want For Her

What kind of person do you want your little sister to become? How do you want her to act and dress? If you want her to be a good person, a Christian light and modest dresser then you have to be all of those things as an example for her. The Bible shows us through people's lives how we are to behave. Christ led a sinless life forgiving those that plotted murder against Him, being kind to everyone He met and quoting scripture when Satan tempted Him. It's easy to forget what someone says; it's much more difficult to forget what they did and how they lived.

In Proverbs 31 we are shown an example of a virtuous woman. Throughout the entire chapter she never says one word, but her actions speak so loudly that all of us today attempt to emulate her example. The woman of Proverbs 31 was first a savvy and resourceful business woman. She not only made clothes and sold them to regular customers; she also made belts and sold them to other merchants, (Prov.31:24). She kept her business expenses low by making her own thread, (Prov. 31:19). Once she'd made a profit she didn't go out and celebrate by splurging on things for herself, she reinvested it in another business opportunity, a vineyard, (Prov. 31:16). While you may have no desire to run a business, good business sense will go a long way in helping you and your little sister. Making and teaching budgeting and doing or making things yourself are all great ways to be virtuous. Her money management skills may have been the chief reason why Prov. 31:11 says, "The heart of her husband safely trusts her; so he will have no lack of gain."

Another reason she was virtuous was because she took care of others and she also took care of herself. Prov. 31:20 says, "She extends her hand to the poor, yes, she reaches out her hands to the needy." In our world of people pretending to be poor and false causes it is prudent to be cautious of every person you and your sister meet with a sign, but that doesn't excuse your responsibility to help those in need. The verse says that the woman of Proverbs 31 is extending her hand and reaching out to others not waiting for someone to ask help of her. Let us be mindful to seek opportunities to show our little sisters how to be kind to the plight of others and to offer help when we can.

Prov. 31:22 says, "She makes tapestry for herself; her clothing is fine linen and purple." This does not sound like a woman who has let herself go. You both should take care of yourselves so that you'll be fit to take care of others. Prov. 31:17 says she strengthens her arms. Eating right, exercising and dressing well will not only make you feel and look your best it will give you the strength to help others achieve their best. Little sisters want to be like their big sisters and this is a great area to encourage her to copy you. May we all learn from the example of the Virtuous woman and find ways to emulate her in our lives.

Help Her Avoid Mistakes You've Made

When you notice your little sister going down a path that you've already been down and you know that path leads to nothing but despair, try and turn her around. Tell her about your experiences in that area, show her any consequences you had to deal with and give her scripture to help her avoid the pitfall. If she has already fallen, encourage and comfort her. Now is not the time to point fingers and ridicule. Give her a shoulder to cry on and an ear to listen. Help her deal with whatever the fallout is and remind her that God still loves her.

The consequences could result from anything like being punished for lying to her parents, spreading gossip or viewing inappropriate material. No matter what it is be a friend, sister and guide and show her a better way of handling temptation. Set up a system so that anytime she feels tempted to do something she can call you or help her memorize a scripture she can repeat to help in difficult situations. I personally love 1. Cor. 10:13, "No temptation has overtaken you except such as is common to man; but God is faithful, who will not allow you to be tempted beyond what you are able, but with the temptation will also make the way of escape, that you may be able to bear it."

Share

Like I mentioned earlier my younger sisters wanted to do everything I did, that included wearing my clothes and jewelry. Your little sister looks up to you for a variety of reasons and I am certain that one of those reasons is because she likes your style. So share a necklace or pair of boots with her; make her feel wanted and treat her like a friend not just someone to give advice to all of the time. You could invite her to a sleep over, play in your closet and with your makeup. Take pictures and have fun. You never know how far a small act of kindness can go and how long it will be remembered.

Your ultimate goal with your little sister is to help her remain close to Christ and in so doing you'll get closer to Christ yourself.

As you can see styling your soul has way more to it than just the clothes you wear; it's about a life committed to Christ, body and soul. But don't let your journey end here come on over to www.virtuousmagazine.com and let's continue our journey together encouraging and building one another up in love and friendship. God bless.

Questions

1. Will you commit to being a big sister?

2. Name one thing you've learned from the Virtuous woman's example that you can apply to your life.

3. How can you share your life experiences with a younger sister to help her remain close to Christ?

"When you learn, *teach*, when you get, *give*." -Maya Angelou

Spread The Love

If you've been inspired, motivated, encouraged or fired up for the Lord here are some easy and loving ways to do as Maya Angelou said and give to others; any of which I will be exceedingly grateful.

1. **Share** the website or a photo of the book on Facebook or Instagram and tag Virtuous Magazine in the post. Write reviews and share quotes.

2. **Tweet** your thoughts or a quote from the book.

3. Send me an **email** with your testimonial, **virtuousmag@yahoo.com.**

4. **Review** the book on Amazon.com or on your own site.

5. **Read** it with friends or use it in your book club.

6. Every article on **virtuousmagazine.com** is free to use. Re-publish and share as you see fit as long as credit and a link back to the site is given.

7. **Remind** your sisters that styling their soul goes way beyond fashion, then use this book as a beacon to light the way!

Can a Magazine *change* the World?

YES IT CAN! Virtuous Magazine is love in action. It's a don't let life happento you magazine for women who want to live intentional and purposeful lives. Visit us today!

www.VirtuousMagazine.com

Special Thanks To:

Breania Owens
Bethany Owens
Lucile Allen
Greg Dismuke
Jonathan Jenkins
Arletha Hutchison
Neadie Dismuke
Alovanni Garrett
Ruby Carr
Kiki Carr
Rodney Carr
Angela Spraggins
Renita Mathis
Rosa Watson
Descygna Webb
Anna Winters
Allen Webster
Brad Harrub
Lynn Manning
and all of the wonderful contributors to Virtuous Magazine!

Thank you!

NOTES

NOTES

NOTES

NOTES

NOTES

Made in the USA
Columbia, SC
25 June 2024